The Nelson Guide to
Research
and Writing
in Political Science

SECOND EDITION

The Nelson Guide to
Research
and Writing
in Political Science

Lucille Charlton
Mount Royal University

Mark Charlton
St. Mary's University College

NELSON / EDUCATION

NELSON / EDUCATION

The Nelson Guide to Research and Writing
in Political Science, Second Edition
by Lucille Charlton and Mark Charlton

Vice President, Editorial
Higher Education:
Anne Williams

Acquisitions Editor:
Anne-Marie Taylor

Marketing Manager:
Ann Byford

Developmental Editor:
Lacey McMaster

Permissions Coordinator:
Vicki Gould

Senior Content Production
Manager:
Imoinda Romain

Production Service:
Cenveo Publisher Services

Copy Editor:
Erin Moore

Proofreader:
Kelli Howey

Production Coordinator:
Ferial Suleman

Design Director:
Ken Phipps

Managing Designer:
Franca Amore

Interior Design:
Dave Murphy

Cover Design:
Trinh Truong

Cover Images:
© VladislavMakarov/
istockphoto (computer key);
© browndogstudios/iStockphoto
(publishing icon)

Compositor:
Cenveo Publisher Services

Printer:
R.R. Donnelley

Library and Archives Canada
Cataloguing in Publication

Charlton, Lucille
    The Nelson guide to resea
and writing in political science /
Lucille Charlton, Mark Charlton.
— 2nd ed.

ISBN 978-0-17-652853-9

    1. Political science—
Authorship. 2. Political science—
Research. 3. Academic writing.
4. Report writing. I. Charlton,
Mark II. Title.

JA86.C43 2013
808'.06632   C2012-90567

ISBN-13: 978-0-17-652853-9
ISBN-10: 0-17-652853-9

Table of Contents

APPENDICES

Introduction

WHAT IS GOOD WRITING
IN POLITICAL SCIENCE?

Politics, from the writing of the earliest Greeks like Plato and Aristotle to contemporary electoral debates, has always been about sharing competing visions of achieving a common good in a society. Explaining and defending ideas have been at the heart of political debate. Whether you are a political candidate running for office, a civil servant in a government department, a researcher at a university, or an ordinary citizen exercising your civic responsibilities, the ability to express yourself clearly and succinctly has always been an essential skill.

Whether or not you are headed for a career in the governmental field, as a student of political science your writing assignments must be more than just a matter of "Can I get a passing grade?" As a student, you are practising professionalism in writing, no matter what the writing assignment is. As in other fields, good writing in political science

- Shows a thorough knowledge of the subject area
- Fulfills the requirements of specific writing assignments
- Combines a well-defined thesis with an appropriate pattern of development
- Supports arguments with ample evidence
- Is mindful of the audience and purpose
- Uses complete and consistent documentation formats
- Looks professional in presentation and format.

Although all writing must meet the same standards of rigour, clarity, and conciseness, good political science writing has the added demands of criticism, analysis, and, at times, a strong tone of persuasiveness. Every political essay should somehow address a "how" or "why" question. Readers should never be left wondering "So what?" at the end of the paper.

If you go on to pursue a career in an area related to political science, you will use your writing skills for a variety of tasks. You might need to prepare a briefing for a minister who is preparing for an upcoming United Nations conference. You may be working for a business organization that sponsors a position paper on discriminatory trade tariffs for a parliamentary hearing.

You might work for an advocacy group and need to prepare a list of policy options for responding to the problems of climate change. As an engaged citizen, you may want to write op-ed articles for a national newspaper.

Each of these examples poses different challenges for the writer, serves a different function, and is aimed at a different audience. Some writing in political science differs significantly from the typical research essay that you may encounter in the classroom situation. An early mastering of these different types of writing assignments will serve you well.

Completing a variety of assignments in political science will not only sharpen your research and writing skills but also prepare you for the different requirements of professional writing demanded on the job. Thus, it is likely that your political science professor will ask you to write different kinds of documents from those you might encounter in other disciplines. The chapters included in this guide will direct you through the essential steps in completing those assignments.

The aim of this guide is not to provide an exhaustive list of resources for good writing techniques but to give you the essential tools for finding further information. Because so much material is now available from electronic sources, the guide contains numerous references to webpages in each section and a comprehensive listing in Appendix I. These webpages are a gateway to more information than can be presented in book format.

HOW TO USE THIS GUIDE

This writer's guide is intended for use in a wide spectrum of political science courses, from introductory to graduate levels. If you are taking your first political science course, read carefully through all the sections, especially those that provide information on how to do research in political science. If you are an upper-level student, skim through the introductory materials and concentrate on the specialized writing assignments in Chapter 4. All students should review the conventions of essay writing and documentation formats presented in Chapter 3 in the section on research documentation.

Throughout Chapter 4, you will find keys to each type of assignment. The keys consolidate essential information about each assignment type and refer you to other information essential for the completion of your assignment. Check these keys before you begin a particular assignment and again at the completion of your first draft, to see whether you have all the essential elements. You will also find suggestions on things to avoid. Check your outline, reread your draft at each stage, and edit your final document to avoid these pitfalls.

Political scientists frequently make presentations or engage in debates. Chapter 5 has extensive information for classroom or public presentations and for debates on current issues. It also includes suggestions for both individual and group work in preparing for oral presentations.

All written work requires careful editing and proofreading. Chapter 6 contains information on writing style, grammar, and mechanics as well as references to popular grammar information websites. Improving your writing style and correcting grammar errors will advance your overall writing skills for any university courses.

The guide also contains FAQ lists and other quick information designed for entry-level political science students. The documentation section gives basic guidelines on the formats for the different styles of documentation. As with all assignments, check with your instructor or teaching assistant if you have questions on the assignments. Whether you are taking your first course in political science or are working on advanced-level courses, this guide to research and writing in political science will assist you with your writing tasks.

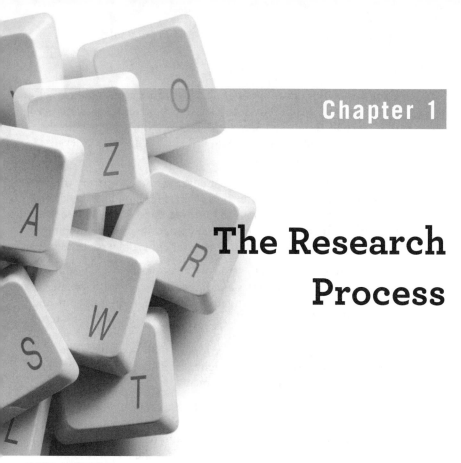

Chapter 1

The Research Process

POLITICAL SCIENCE AS A FIELD OF STUDY

As a field of academic discipline, political science is highly eclectic and diverse. No one common approach or methodology exists for the study of politics. Political scientists themselves disagree intensely on the appropriate methodological tools for studying the discipline, the ideas represented by various schools of thought, and even the definition of politics itself. This diversity of views and approaches makes political science a fascinating subject to study and debate.

Political science encompasses several subfields or specializations. These specializations can, in part, be identified by the way the Canadian Political Science Association (CPSA) structures its annual meetings, where political scientists from across Canada and from other countries gather to present the findings of their research. The call for papers for the CPSA annual meetings identifies 12 different categories in which papers will be presented, providing a quick snapshot of the various subfields within the discipline:

1. **Canadian politics** examines political institutions and political behaviour in Canada. Political science associations in other countries, such as the United States or Great Britain, would similarly focus on the study of the national institutions and processes in their own political systems.

2. **Comparative politics** focuses on analyzing and comparing the political systems of two countries, such as Canada and the United States. Common subdivisions in this area are comparing one industrialized nation to another and comparing two developing countries to see how they deal with political problems differently.

3. **International relations** is the study of relations between nation-states as well as the activities and interactions of international organizations, such as the United Nations, and non-governmental organizations, like the Red Cross. In the past, the study of international relations focused primarily on the issues of war and peace. Now, it increasingly covers other topics, such as global political economy, international human rights, trans-border environmental issues, poverty, and underdevelopment.

4. **Local and urban politics** focuses on the study of political institutions and political behaviour at the municipal and local levels. Although this area is often underrated and receives less attention than do other fields of political science, it is the level of political activity that students may have greatest access to for firsthand study.

5. **Political behaviour/sociology** deals primarily with the search for explanations of particular types of political behaviour, such as voting patterns and trends in political participation. This subfield often draws heavily from the insights and methodology of psychology and sociology.

6. **Political economy** examines the interaction between economic forces and political behaviour and how they shape public policies. This subfield emphasizes the close link between politics and economics.

7. **Political theory** analyzes the fundamental concepts of politics and poses many of the critical "great questions" that underlie political debate: What is justice? What is democracy? How should the individual relate to the state? The study of political theory may encompass both an explanation of how these fundamental questions relate to contemporary problems and the historical evolution and transformation of these concepts.

8. **Provincial and territorial politics** studies the role of political institutions and processes at the level of provincial and territorial governments. Other nations, such as the United States, have their own equivalent levels.

9. **Public administration** studies the way that government policies are implemented, giving particular attention to the inner workings of governmental bureaucracies.

10. **Law and public policy** examines the interaction of law and the courts with other institutions in the political process. An example would be a study of how the Supreme Court of Canada influences the laws made by Parliament.

11. **Race, ethnicity, indigenous peoples, and politics** focuses on the development and analysis of public policy pertaining to minority, ethnic, and Aboriginal groups.

12. **Women, gender, and politics** studies the role of gender in the political arena and how gender issues shape political processes.

As with any area of study, some of these subfields overlap in their interests. Another way of investigating the specialized areas of political science is to look at upper-level and graduate courses offered at many universities.

GETTING STARTED IN RESEARCH

Whether you are attending classes at a large university or a smaller community college, taking your first course in political science can be challenging if you are unfamiliar with the available resources. Before you begin your first assignment in political science, check out what services are available at your institution. Finding out how to access resources quickly now will save time when you are working on research and writing. Taking a workshop on library research is one way to get started on your research project.

Gathering information on resources includes all of the following:

University or college resources

- Hours of the writing centre
- Hours tutors are available and how to contact them
- Information on writing workshops or other assistance available to students
- Library website address and links for documentation and research assistance

Instructor or teaching assistant

- Course website
- Instructor's or assistant's office hours
- Online or e-mail assistance instructions (For example, does the instructor require 48 hours' notice for answering queries? Will he or she answer e-mail on weekends?)

ONLINE RESOURCES FOR WRITING

Your next step is to become familiar with the websites for writing, research, and citation styles listed in Appendix I: Sources to Consult. Look through the materials in the "Information on Writing, Research, and Citation Styles" section in Appendix I, and bookmark the ones you feel are most useful.

ASSIGNMENT ANALYSIS

When you receive your assignment, start by reading through the instructions carefully. You will need to answer the following questions before starting the research:

1. What type of assignment is it (essay, book review, or position paper)?

2. What keywords describe the assignment (analyzing, describing, comparing, persuading)?

3. What citation style is required (APA, MLA, or other)?

4. What is the time frame (due dates for proposals, outlines, and final drafts)?

Jot down any questions you have about the assignment, and consult your instructor.

Your next step is to set up a schedule for completing the various components of your paper. Allow time for (1) researching, (2) organizing, writing, and editing at least three drafts, (3) consulting with tutors or instructors, and (4) finishing. Be sure to allow extra time just before the assignment is due in case you run into difficulties in completing the work. You want to avoid last-minute problems.

EVALUATING RESEARCH MATERIALS

Before beginning any assignment in political science, you need to be clear about the different types of resource materials available. In the area of politics, you will find an abundance of documents for research. In fact, on some topics, you may find far more material than you can possibly read, especially for a short essay. You will need to distinguish between primary and secondary sources, primary and secondary research, and scholarly and popular resources. After you learn about the different types of resources and how to find them, you will be ready to work on your first research essay in political science.

PRIMARY VERSUS SECONDARY SOURCES

Researchers distinguish between primary and secondary sources. **Primary sources** are materials that are written or produced by people who are directly involved in the topic under study. These might include diaries, autobiographies, memoirs, or speeches. Primary resources also include reports of meetings, such as records of parliamentary debates and committee hearings; official reports of governmental agencies and organizations; treaties between nations; statutes and court judgments; and government data, such as census data or immigration statistics. Contemporary coverage of an event, such as newspaper or magazine descriptions of a convention to select a party leader, is also a primary source.

While upper-level courses and research done for a thesis will require greater attention to primary resources, research work for undergraduate courses in political science also relies on secondary sources. However, for any essays, do not overlook the value of primary resources, if available. For example, if you are writing an argumentative essay on whether Canada should continue its military commitment to NATO, you might want to read the speeches of Members of Parliament who have debated this issue in the past. These speeches may provide some useful quotations in support of your argument or give you a sense of the arguments and counterarguments that were raised in the heat of public debate.

The task of accessing primary resources has become much easier with many records becoming available online. The records of parliamentary and congressional proceedings are easily searchable through keyword and subject functions. Many international organizations also have their public record of deliberations and reports available online. Canadian government agencies such as Statistics Canada and Elections Canada make their data available directly through online access.

Secondary sources are materials written by scholars or specialists who are interpreting an event or providing an in-depth analysis of primary resources. For example, a journal article analyzing the evolving nature of leadership conventions in Canadian politics is a secondary source. Good secondary sources rely on an analysis of primary sources, so the journal article would be based on interviews with those involved in the leadership conventions, eyewitness observations by the researcher, and memoirs or autobiographies of leadership candidates.

Even if you plan to use primary sources for part of your research, every good research project begins with a review of what has already been written on the topic in the secondary literature. A good place to start is in your course textbook or reader. The authors may have included sources for further study of an issue. Use footnotes and references lists to find other material on your subject. You can access secondary material through university library catalogues and database indexes, described below.

PRIMARY RESEARCH VERSUS SECONDARY RESEARCH

A further distinction can be drawn between primary research and secondary research.

Primary research presents the original findings of a research project for the first time. For example, a researcher may be studying how and if attitudes toward the homeless are changing. She would conduct a survey, analyze the results, and publish them in an appropriate journal. Such primary research material is usually found in scholarly journals or books published by academic publishers, or published directly by research institutes or government agencies that have sponsored the research. The researchers of these articles give firsthand observations, explain the proof for their theories, and detail their methodology.

Secondary research does not present any new research findings; rather, it is a compilation or evaluation of previously published research. Secondary research is typically found in textbooks, encyclopaedias, and some newspaper or magazine articles. Online sources can provide facts, opinions, and analysis of current events. How much you use secondary research material will depend on the nature of your writing assignment. If you are writing an argumentative essay on a current, hotly debated topic, you may find that secondary research sources will give you a good summary of the issues. However, if you are writing a research-oriented paper, you will want to focus mostly on primary research, since these materials are likely to give a more accurate description of both the research findings and the methodology. Although online sources or your class textbook may give you some useful background about your topic, be sure to investigate other sources. Citing *Wikipedia* or political blogs like *Canadian Soapbox* as major sources for your essay tells your professor that you have not done much serious research!

Literature reviews are another valuable source of secondary research material. A thorough literature review both lists existing literature on a topic and comments critically on how the research adds to an understanding of the field. Although not considered primary research by themselves, literature reviews can be valuable because they can direct you to the most significant studies on the topic you are investigating. In addition, literature reviews often point out areas where more research and study is needed. Thus, students looking for a topic for a major research paper or thesis can get a sense of what new research needs to be done.

SCHOLARLY VERSUS POPULAR SOURCES

A third useful distinction to keep in mind is the difference between popular and scholarly resources. A **scholarly journal** is one published by and for specialists and experts in a given field. Articles in these journals usually report on primary research projects or provide a review of the research literature on a specific topic. In addition, most scholarly journals have an extensive book review section in which specialists comment on the relevance of new books in the field. Some scholarly journals, such as the *Canadian Journal of Political Science* or the *American Political Science Review,* carry articles from all fields of study in political science. Others, such as *International Studies Quarterly* or *Political Theory,* publish articles only in the subfield of political science included in their titles.

Scholarly journals are important because of the rigorous review process by which articles are selected for publication. Before publication, experts in the field evaluate each work according to exacting academic and scholarly standards. Articles are not published unless they make some new contribution to the research and understanding of a topic. Thus, the reader is assured that the articles appearing in these journals have met a certain standard of research excellence. The publishers require a description of the research methods used, careful documentation, and a bibliography of all the sources used in writing the article. These journals are usually referred to as **peer-reviewed** or **refereed journals.**

In contrast, **popular sources,** such as newsmagazines, are written for a broad public audience. The articles are usually written by staff writers employed by the magazine or by freelance writers who are paid per article. Although some journalists may specialize in covering politics, their coverage of political events is more immediate and less geared to giving an in-depth analysis and perspective that would be considered primary research. Unlike scholarly journals, news articles are not reviewed by specialists or experts in the field before they are published. Journalists for these publications are writing to please a readership, not to meet the research standards of an academic community. As a result, editorial standards and expectations differ significantly among popular publications. Popular news stories neither mention how the information was gathered nor provide citations of sources that the reader can follow up on; therefore, treat material from popular sources with some caution.

Some exceptions do exist. A number of magazines and newspapers specialize in longer, in-depth articles on specific issues, sometimes based on extensive research by the author. In some cases, the writers are experts or academics who have already published their research in scholarly journals but now want to reach a broader audience. Their work provides a good introduction to and summary of various issues. A few newspapers present themselves as "national" newspapers and aspire to be newspapers of "record"—that is, they hope to provide a fairly comprehensive and authoritative record of events of national and international importance. Magazines may present themselves more as opinion leaders, appealing to a more thoughtful audience. Some of the magazines and newspapers that often carry more in-depth articles are listed in Appendix I: Sources to Consult at the end of this guide. You can access national newspapers and newsmagazines in the current periodical section of university libraries or by checking online versions. Also, search for the *Canadian Newsstand* database through your university library. It contains a large collection of current newspaper and magazine publications.

The same distinction made between popular and scholarly sources can also be applied to books. When evaluating the usefulness of a book for research on your selected topic, pay careful attention to both the author and the publisher. Is the author a specialist associated with a university or research institute? Is the book published by an academic or university press? Academic publications usually go through the same rigorous peer-review process as articles in scholarly journals.

Be aware that some books may be self-published or published by a so-called vanity press, which charges authors to have their books published. Other self-published books and materials appear on the Internet. These books have not undergone any peer-review process and therefore need to be treated much more critically before being cited in your research.

Don't overlook collections of articles and essays, often referred to as "readers." Used as supplementary texts for courses, readers include collections of articles from a range of sources covering the topics studied in your course. Because the articles have been carefully selected to cover the main themes, they can provide an excellent starting point for your research, especially in introductory courses.

USING LIBRARY RESOURCES

Now that you have a sense of the various types of research materials available to you, you are ready to begin looking for resources for your essay. With the availability of the Internet, the temptation in beginning a paper is to start with an Internet search using a search engine such as Google or

Bing and then print the first half-dozen sources that you find. Although this might get you a passing grade on a short essay in an introductory class, it will not enable you to meet the standards for a more substantial essay, particularly as you move along in your political science program.

Despite the convenience of the Internet, the best place to begin your research remains your university library. With the computerization of library catalogues and online accessibility from home, your research task can be both faster and more fruitful than in the past. Your library's web-page not only provides you access to its online catalogue of books but also offers you an array of electronic periodical indexes and databases that you can access online. In addition, you can read what are referred to as "full-text" versions of journal articles and even save them to your computer.

Your search for research material should begin with books. Then look at articles in scholarly journals and relevant magazines. Then broaden your search to websites sponsored by government or reputable organizations. Using a combination of sources shows thorough and professional research.

FINDING BOOKS

Even though online library catalogues vary from one institution to another, they all have common features. The quickest way to search for books is by author or title. Perhaps your professor has recommended a particular author in class or made passing reference to the title of a book on your topic. Keying in the author or title will reveal not only the particular reference but also possible links to other pertinent information. If you don't have a specific title, search for a keyword or more general subject. Then use the advanced search feature to add more keywords, making your search more specific.

Suppose you have decided to write a paper on the role of Stephen Harper as prime minister. Typing in "Stephen Harper" in the title, keyword, or subject search may result in the following catalogue entry:

Title	Harperland: the politics of control
Author	Martin, Lawrence
Publisher	Toronto: Viking, 2010
Description	301 p.
ISBN	978070065172
Subjects	Harper, Stephen, 1959
	Canada—Politics and government
	Executive Power

The catalogue entry gives you a basic description of the book. Click on the author's name to see what other books the author has published. Perhaps Lawrence Martin has published other books on Canadian government that would be helpful to your essay. Entries may contain a list of the Table of Contents for this book. Glancing through the contents will show you specifically which chapters are pertinent to your research. Some results may show only one or two chapters in a book focusing on your topic, so you should still consider checking on these sources. You will also note under the Subjects category the additional links to books specifically on Canadian government and Stephen Harper. Clicking on these will provide additional lists of books to browse through.

Many online library catalogues will allow you to click on a button, such as "add to my list." When you have completed your search, you can create a document of all your titles. You can then cut and paste these into your research bibliography or print out the list—including the library call numbers—to help you find the books once you go to the library.

Do not forget to check other entries from your initial search. Many library holdings are now in electronic format, so check with your library to access these documents.

FINDING ARTICLES IN PERIODICALS

Once you have identified book resources, it is time to move on to periodical articles. Periodical articles are shorter pieces of writing that appear in journals or magazines that are published on a regular basis. The distinctions made earlier between scholarly and popular publications are of particular importance in your search during this phase.

Your task is made easier by the fact that university libraries provide a variety of databases that can be searched online. Libraries usually group their databases by disciplinary areas, allowing you to access those that are most relevant to your field of research. A major advantage of library-accessed databases is that most now offer direct access to full-text versions of articles. Some full-text databases include both html and pdf versions of articles. Choose pdf versions whenever possible because they include unchanging page numbers that are easier to cite. Full-text versions allow you to read the article immediately, save it to a file, or send it to your e-mail account. If the full text is not available, read through the abstract if available to see if the article is relevant. The "find full text" feature in library services will help you locate a full text of the article online, in print, or through library loan. Some citations also provide direct links to other resources on the same topic.

To acquaint yourself with the prominent journals in political science, scan through the various database holdings in political science, or go online directly for individual journals. You will discover a variety of political science journals. Some, like the *Canadian Journal of Political Science* or the *American Political Science Review*, are general in nature, carrying articles from a range of political science subfields. Others, like *Political Theory* or *International Studies Quarterly,* focus on a particular subfield of the discipline. For a list of some of the more prominent journals in political science, consult Appendix I: Sources to Consult at the end of this guide.

For research in political science, some of the more relevant online databases you should look for are as follows:

- Academic Search Complete (EBSCOhost)
- Canadian Newsstand
- CBCA Reference (Canadian Business and Current Affairs)
- CIAO: Columbia International Affairs Online
- IPSA: International Political Science Abstracts
- Sage Full-Text Collections

These databases allow you to do a variety of searches by author, periodical, subject, or keyword. By using the advanced search functions, you can limit your search to a more manageable size. Many of these databases have a box that you can click to limit your search to peer-reviewed journals. This is an excellent way to narrow your search to scholarly journals and avoid long lists of articles that appear in the popular media.

USING INTERNET RESOURCES

Once you have completed the first two stages, you are ready to begin searching the broader ranges of resources available through the Internet. The easiest way to begin your search on the Internet is to use one of the popular search engines, such as Google, Bing, or Yahoo! Instead of searching for a general topic, use these general search engines to find websites for specific organizations or government publications. Fortunately for political science researchers, many United Nations agencies, governments, non-governmental organizations, advocacy groups, and political parties make their materials available electronically to the broader public. For example, searching for the government of New Brunswick will locate its official site. From there, you can look for news releases, business policies, or any other topics relating to provincial matters.

ASSESSING INTERNET SOURCES

Although the Internet gives you fast and easy access to an enormous amount of potential research material, Internet research poses some unique challenges in terms of evaluating the quality of your resources. The material in scholarly books and journals has passed a strict process of peer evaluation before appearing in print. In addition, published academic writing always tries to document clearly the sources for claims made in the research. Anyone doubting the veracity of a claim can check the sources cited to see whether there is a basis for the conclusions drawn.

In contrast, almost anyone can post material on the Internet, partly because of the affordability of websites and the ease with which they can be established. In many cases, it is not clear who wrote the material or where the research came from. Before using Internet material in your research, it is important to carefully assess its quality.

Internet materials fall into several categories. Some materials that you access on the Internet are simply electronic versions of articles available in print form. In cases of government documents or articles from a peer-reviewed scholarly journal, such as the *Canadian Journal of Political Science* or the *American Political Science Review,* use the same evaluation standards as you would for any published document.

Because of the high costs of printing and longer time to reach publication, some academics are beginning to publish e-journals rather than the traditional print versions. E-journals function like traditional academic journals, with a rigorous peer-review process before articles are accepted for publication. The e-journals meet the same high academic standards of traditional journals, although they are available *only* in electronic format. It is important to check the information on the homepage to verify how articles are selected for publication. A peer-reviewed journal always carries greater credibility than a non-peer-reviewed journal does.

Ask some key questions when evaluating the usefulness and reliability of Internet resources:

- Who is the author? Is his or her identity clearly stated? Does the author have the academic credentials or experience to write on this particular topic? What is his or her institutional affiliation? Is the author connected with a university, research institution, or some government or non-governmental agency?

- If the author is associated with a particular group, do you know something about this group? Is he or she affiliated with particular interests or a particular point of view? What kind of reputation does the author have?

- If assertions or claims are made on the website, are the sources of this information or claims identified? Are they presented in a way that you can follow up to verify the authenticity?

- Has the information on the website been updated recently?

The following websites are very helpful for evaluating web sources:

Dalhousie University Library Checklist
http://libraries.dal.ca/using_the_library/tutorials/evaluating_web_
resources/website_checklist.html

University of California at Berkeley: Evaluating Webpages
http://www.lib.berkeley.edu/TeachingLib/Guides/Internet/Evaluate.html

GATEWAYS FOR POLITICAL SCIENCE

An alternative to beginning your search with a general search engine is to use one of the "gateway" sites that provide guidance in looking for resources on the Internet. The advantage of these sites is that they often classify resources by type, making it easier to narrow your search.

Some recommended gateway political science websites include the following:

CyberSciencesPo: A French-language site at the University of Ottawa
http://aix1.uottawa.ca/~fgingras/cyber/scipol.html#canassociations

General Guide to Canadian Politics
http://www.politicalresources.net/canada/canada.htm

Internet Resources for Political Science, University of Windsor
http://web2.uwindsor.ca/courses/ps/dartnell/index.html

Library and Archives Canada: Political Science
http://www.collectionscanada.gc.ca/caninfo/ep032.htm

Richard Kimber's Political Science Resources
http://www.psr.keele.ac.uk

University of British Columbia
http://toby.library.ubc.ca/subjects/subjpage2.cfm?id=169

In addition, some websites allow you to search for documents within particular international and governmental agencies. A few good starting points are listed here.

Canada Government Websites

http://search-recherche.gc.ca

Use keywords to search all the websites related to the Canadian government.

Canadian Parliamentary Business and Publications Search Engine

http://www.parl.gc.ca/search/search_main.asp?Language=
E&Parl=37&Ses=2

Use keywords to search the records of the House of Commons and Senate.

Canadian Supreme Court

http://www.lexum.org/csc-scc/en/index.html

Provides the full text online of all decisions of the Canadian Supreme Court; can be searched using keywords, participating parties, judges present, or authors cited.

European Union

http://europa.eu/index_en.htm

Fedworld Homepage

http://www.fedworld.gov

Provides an entry point to all United States federal government resources, including U.S. Supreme Court decisions.

United Nations Web Search

http://www.un.org/search/

Entry to the entire UN system and links to all UN organizational websites.

Many government agencies now make many of their databases available online. Although in some cases there may be additional access fees, most make the popular databases or digests of important data collections available for free. Two good places to look for Canadian databases are as follows:

Government Publications Canada

http://www.publications.gc.ca

Statistics Canada

http://www.statcan.gc.ca

 Keys to good research

- Use your institution's library catalogue and databases
- Attend a workshop from your library on how to do research
- Be specific in your search, using keywords and gateways to your subject area
- Evaluate material for reliability
- Ask for assistance

 Avoid

- General Internet searches that waste time
- Outdated or unreliable resources

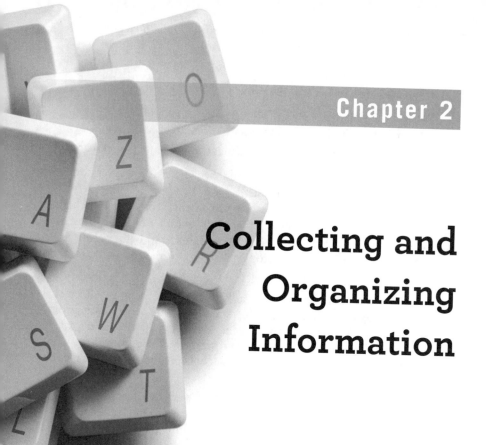

© malerapaso/iStockphoto

Chapter 2

Collecting and Organizing Information

FROM TOPIC TO PRELIMINARY THESIS

The topic and thesis of your essay are central to the tasks of collecting and organizing information. The **topic** is the broad subject area; the **thesis** is the controlling idea of the essay, which offers your perspective on a question or a problem. The topic directs you to the first stages of research, whereas the thesis determines how you will structure or outline your work. Every part of the finished essay supports the central thesis statement.

CHOOSING AND DEVELOPING A TOPIC

Some instructors require students to write on a predetermined topic, while others give only general directions for an essay. If you don't receive any specific instructions, you can choose and develop a general topic into a coherent, supportable thesis statement by following some basic steps:

- Brainstorming
- Choosing a general area of interest
- Doing the initial research

- Narrowing the focus of the topic
- Deciding on the attitude or perspective
- Completing additional, more focused research
- Writing a preliminary thesis statement to guide further research

Note: Your final thesis statement should be written only after thorough revision and editing of your first draft.

These steps do not necessarily happen in the same order each time. Some students like to brainstorm the topic before doing any research; others conduct some broad sweeps of research material before using brainstorming techniques. For general topics, use any of the following methods of brainstorming to generate an ideas list:

- **Lists.** On a blank paper, write a list of as many ideas as you can about the topic. Perhaps you have already done some reading for your class or heard a lecture on the topic. As you look over your list, highlight important points and start organizing details or subordinate points. Cross out those concepts that do not fit into the topic after further consideration.
- **Word circles.** Write the main topic in the centre of a sheet of paper. Brainstorm other concepts, ideas, and areas to explore. Connect similar ideas with lines to show relationships.
- **Discussion.** Work with a partner to discuss ideas. Take notes. Highlight and number similar ideas that can be developed.

For any research paper, brainstorming is only a start. After a brainstorming session, it's time to conduct some initial research on your topic. Use your brainstorming ideas as a start, but do not limit the ideas for the thesis until you have done your preliminary research. Then it will be easy to add to your ideas list and organize your research information.

The stages of developing a final thesis statement might look something like this:

- Topic assigned by the instructor: *Canada's immigration policy.*
- My area of interest in this topic: *The effects of immigration on the economy.*
- Preliminary research: *Read several articles for background information.*
- Attitude/perspective on topic: *Favourable to an open immigration policy.*
- Preliminary thesis statement: *An open immigration policy promotes a healthy economy.* This statement needs detailed support, so start asking questions: *How? Why? What areas need research?*

- Research areas needed to support thesis: *(1) Numbers of immigrants in the past 10 years, (2) sectors of the economy that have benefited from immigration, (3) settlement patterns, (4) costs to the government for implementing changes, (5) benefits the immigrants themselves receive, (6) population growth rates.*
- Refine/change thesis after research: After more research, you may decide to change the topic drastically. For example, you could decide that open immigration is actually detrimental rather than beneficial. Another direction might be to discuss the pros and cons of Canada's immigration policy.

At this point, it is important to settle on your controlling idea so that you can focus your research. Remember, a good thesis statement is narrow; it does not try to encompass too large a discussion for the scope of the paper. Concentrating on the thesis statement guides you to further refine the research areas in pursuit of material to support your principal arguments. The key word in developing a thesis is flexibility. As your research progresses, you may need to add or discard ideas. Evaluate your thesis in light of your research: narrow the ideas, throw out points that can't be supported, and dig out more research in a particular area. If you are not familiar with how to do advanced searches to focus on a particular area, ask for assistance from your institution's library services.

Many students have no trouble finding sufficient source materials for a research essay. However, they are soon overwhelmed by the amount of materials and have difficulty knowing just how to take notes on or organize what they have found. If you have done some brainstorming and idea generation, look for points that fall together, contrasts that can be made, or causes and effects of a particular problem. Having both a preliminary thesis and a skeleton outline in mind will give you an idea of where to start with taking notes on your research materials.

Researchers use various methods of taking notes and organizing information. The key elements to keep in mind are recording, analyzing, organizing, and citing.

Recording your notes is just taking notes on or making an electronic copy of what you want to keep for your research. The next step is **analyzing** the information—that is, thinking it through, processing what you have found, making connections with other pieces of information, and writing down your critical responses. The third key component is **organizing** your findings into categories or subheadings for each part of your essay. The final key element is accurately **citing** each of the sources you have found. You must be able to find that material again and direct your reader to the source when you use a quotation, paraphrase, or summary of another person's work.

RECORDING

As you find resources, you need to keep track of both print and electronic documents. First, deal with longer print documents like books and journal articles by deciding which parts of the document are relevant to your work. For example, if you find a book on your topic but think only one chapter is relevant, you may wish to photocopy just that chapter. However, for longer print documents, taking notes in a notebook or on the computer is the best way to retain important information. Work through a longer document by summarizing sections, typing out possible important quotations, and paraphrasing pertinent material. Keep careful track of all page numbers for your citations. If you already have a rough outline of your essay, create separate sections with appropriate headings for your notes. For example, if you are writing on the topic of immigration, your notes on how open immigration benefits the economy can all be saved under the topic "benefits." Sorting notes and information at this stage will save time later.

Electronic documents can be collected in different ways. If you are using a pdf file, the entire article should be saved to your computer. If you find an article or report in html format, the entire article should be copy and saved or create a file of URL links for documents from stable sources. Save the complete article, even if you think you will only use a part of it. You may find that you need more complete information at a later stage. Remember that some citation styles require access dates for web material, so note the date you view or download these files.

Create files by topic and make sure you back up all research and writing materials. Many electronic articles have the complete reference at the top or bottom of the page; if not, you should add source information both to the file and to your bibliography. Record access dates and database information as required by the citation style you are using. Avoid copying chunks of articles into your notes without exact citations. Keep adding all references to your working bibliography as you find material, even if you don't end up using everything in the final version.

✓ Keys for research

- Understand the types of sources required for the assignment
- Check a variety of sources
- Develop a working thesis and rough outline early in the research process
- Evaluate sources for reliability
- Keep careful records of all sources

Avoid

- Over reliance on one source
- Searches that are too general and return hundreds of documents

ANALYZING INFORMATION

As you start saving research materials, decide how best to make analytic notes for both print and electronic documents. Don't assume that you will remember all the points of each item you have read. Whether you are working with print or electronic documents, plan to complete these basic steps to analyze your material.

- **Read carefully.** If you have just skimmed through the material, go back and do a complete, detailed reading.

- **Annotate.** Highlight quotations, mark sections for paraphrasing, note important facts, and make notes in the margins for ideas to explore or questions about the material. Annotations can be done by hand on print copies or electronically using a variety of programs such as Microsoft Word or GoodReader. Do not over annotate. Too many highlights or margin notes can be confusing at a later point. Keep annotations to the point.

- **Summarize.** Always summarize the material in your own words. What is the main argument? How does this information support points you are making?

- **Divide.** Start dividing the material into sections that fit into your outline. Keep a master outline and note which items are best to support your arguments. Make notes on which sections of your rough outline need more information or analysis.

Don't forget to back up all electronic documents and notes.

 Keys to analyzing information

- Read for main ideas
- Reread for details
- Annotate each resource
- Summarize in your own words

 Avoid

- Over annotating
- Copy and paste methods that lose track of citations

ORGANIZING AND OUTLINING YOUR FINDINGS

As you collect and analyze your materials, you need to organize your research and move from a rough to a more detailed outline. Do you have sufficient materials to support your point of view? Are your resources up-to-date? As you work, check some of the writing guides mentioned and begin forming an organizational structure for the essay. You may need to go back and refine the thesis statement, clarify the assignment, or look for different kinds of supporting evidence.

You will probably gather much more information than you can use in your essay. One way to determine what information you will use to support your thesis is by designating points as major, minor, or marginal. A major point of support is one that is essential to your arguments. A minor supporting point can be left in or taken out, depending on development of the text. You might want to include it in the first draft, and then edit as needed. A marginal piece of information is either redundant, nonessential to the argument, or does not support the argument at all.

At this point, do not delete or trash the notes and analyses you made. You might need to reevaluate the worth of the points by asking the following questions:

- Do I need more information on this particular point (more research)?
- Does this point belong in another section of the text (reorganize)?
- Does this point illustrate an opposing argument to my thesis? Don't leave out points because you don't agree with them. In some types of essays, it's important to acknowledge the opposing views. (See "Argumentative Writing and Issue Reaction Papers" in Chapter 4.)

As you refine your rough outline, determine which structural elements you need to incorporate to organize your arguments:

- **Definition:** Define what something is or how you will use a term in your writing.
- **Chronology:** Relate a series of events in chronological order. Good transitions (first, second, third) are essential.
- **Description or process:** Explain how a process works, such as the process of a bill becoming a law.
- **Examples and illustrations:** Give a detailed example of a concept or idea.
- **Comparison or contrast:** Show how things are alike or different and comment on why these comparisons are significant.

- **Classification/division:** Divide a topic into logical subgroups and discuss each one.

- **Cause and effect:** Show what causes something or what the effects of something are. Essays can focus mainly on the causes or mainly on the effects. For example, one essay might thoroughly describe the causes of the health care crisis, while another might look at the effects of government cutbacks on health care.

- **Analysis/criticism:** Examine an issue, problem, or event and propose solutions.

Look through your notes and develop a detailed outline, starting with the major ideas of the thesis statement. Leave plenty of space under each major heading. Start adding the supporting arguments in point form. Look for major support points and minor supplementary details. This outline will form the body of your essay.

After you have a first draft of the body, add ideas for the introduction and conclusion, and then return to your preliminary thesis. Now it's time to reevaluate and rewrite the thesis, taking into account all the research support you have discovered.

Let's return for a moment to the preliminary thesis stated in the assignment on Canada's immigration policy.

The preliminary thesis statement was that "an open immigration policy promotes a healthy economy." In looking over the thesis, you would probably decide that the question of "how" is the most important. Your research has turned up several ideas that answer the question of how, including that an open immigration policy creates a higher demand for consumer goods, a greater number of successful entrepreneurs, and a larger tax base for the government. You can fill in details to support each of these major points.

An outline for the essay might look something like this:

Introduction: (leave details until later)

Thesis statement: *An open immigration policy promotes a healthy economy.*

Major points:

1. A brief overview of the history of immigration policy (chronological)

2. Immigrants create a higher demand for consumer goods (These next three sections are classifications, or divisions of the major point into logical parts and discussing them.)

   2.1 Bring more money into economy

   2.2 Many immigrant families have more than one person working

   2.3 Another point needed?

---

3. Immigrant entrepreneurs contribute to local economies

   3.1 Statistics on amounts of capital investments

   3.2 Data on immigrant employers and job creation

4. Immigrants contribute to the tax base

   4.1 Statistics on first- and second-generation employment

   4.2 Numbers of immigrant professionals entering workforce

   4.3 Government figures on the overall cost of immigration

Conclusion: Canada benefits from having an open immigration policy.

At this point, you may wish to consult with your instructor. Ask if your research and outline include all the major ideas necessary for a complete analysis of your topic. Your instructor may suggest other sources to consult, changes to the order of the outline, or revisions to the thesis.

After determining a more detailed outline, you can reorganize your notes, fill in the details of supporting evidence for each area, and decide on your opening and closing statements.

Now you are ready to refine your thesis statement. Write out several versions, choosing the one that most clearly states both your analysis of the problem and how your essay will discuss it. The thesis on immigration might evolve something like this:

Preliminary: *An open immigration policy promotes a healthy economy.* This statement doesn't tell the reader how you are going to discuss the topic.

Another draft: *There are three major ways that an open immigration policy promotes a healthy economy.* This statement encompasses the idea of three divisions, but it doesn't tell the reader what the divisions are.

A third version: *Although some people object to open immigration, an open-door policy has significant benefits for the Canadian economy.* "Some people" is too vague, and you are giving the objections central focus at the beginning of the essay.

Final version: *An open immigration policy benefits the Canadian economy by creating higher consumer demand, encouraging more entrepreneurs, and increasing tax revenues.*

This version

- states your main topic: open immigration
- clearly shows your attitude: benefits

- sets out three areas of discussion: consumer demand, entrepreneurs, and tax revenues

After creating the final version of your thesis statement, go back to your outline and add details, making sure your points follow a logical order. If you have changed your thesis significantly, such as preferring to compare the pros and cons of immigration, you will have to rewrite your outline and research different kinds of information.

Go back through your outline and supporting points and decide what visuals may work to support your ideas. Visuals include any charts, graphs, tables, or images. For example, you may decide the best way to support your thesis is to create a table showing the immigration numbers over the past 10 years. You may use visuals directly from your research sources, or you may create your own from information you have found. In either case, you must cite sources just like you would for a quotation. Check the general writing sources in this book for more information on what kind of visual works best and how citations must be done.

 Keys to organizing and outlining

- Develop a detailed outline
- Make changes to your outline as you find more information
- Check for logical development and transitions
- Relate all discussion to supporting main thesis

 Avoid

- Discussion that is off the topic
- Setting out details before main ideas

DEVELOPING A WORKING BIBLIOGRAPHY

Right from the start of your research project, you must pay careful attention to all the details in the note-taking, quoting, and documenting of your research findings. Failure to accurately document your sources in the research and note-taking phases can cause problems in the final stages of compiling a list of references.

Accurate documentation fills two important functions in research and writing: (1) attributing material to its original author and (2) enabling the reader to consult the documents used in the research.

Readers of research papers expect

- credit to be given for all quotes, paraphrases, summaries, and visuals
- accurate and consistent bibliographic information

If you are not familiar with basic documentation styles, check the examples of citation formats and the information in Chapter 3 before you begin your first research paper assignment.

Here are some basic steps to follow for creating a working bibliography.

1. Determine which format of documentation is required for the assignment. Some courses/instructors prefer a certain style, such as that of the American Psychological Association (APA), the Modern Language Association (MLA), or the Chicago Manual of Style (CMS). If you are not certain which format to use, check with your instructor. Some courses may require you to follow institutional guidelines or style sheets.

2. Before beginning your research, set up a bibliography document on your computer. As you research your subject, enter all necessary information for each source into your bibliography, even if you're not sure whether you will use that source. Use this information to create citations within the essay and a works cited list. If you cut and paste citations directly from the reference, make sure you have all the information you need. For example, APA lists only the first initial, not the first name of an author. If you are using Chicago or MLA, you will need the complete first name. MLA style requires the name of the database, so record which one you are using. Library record pages from electronic catalogues may contain a ready-made citation in the correct style. You may cut and paste these references, but always check for accuracy and correct formatting before using for your final copy. If you are using a website as a source, include the complete URL for now and access date. You may not need it in the final reference list.

If you are working on a longer research project, you might want to add informal annotations to your bibliographic entry. Your annotations will remind you of the significance of a particular work and make it easier to sift through large amounts of material. Some researchers keep a permanent computer file on research citations with annotations for future use. (See "Compiling an Annotated Bibliography" in Chapter 4.)

Your working bibliography may grow quite large, but as you skim through materials, you will probably quickly eliminate those that are not pertinent to your topic. Do not delete these entries from your bibliography right away. Create a secondary or "maybe" section or file and shift those entries to it. You might change your mind and come back to them later.

✓ Keys to developing a working bibliography

- Accurately document all research materials in the required citation style
- Categorize your findings and sort by importance
- Use annotations to help you remember the material
- Keep a backup of all your work

✗ Avoid

- Inconsistent documentation
- Sloppy recordkeeping that wastes time

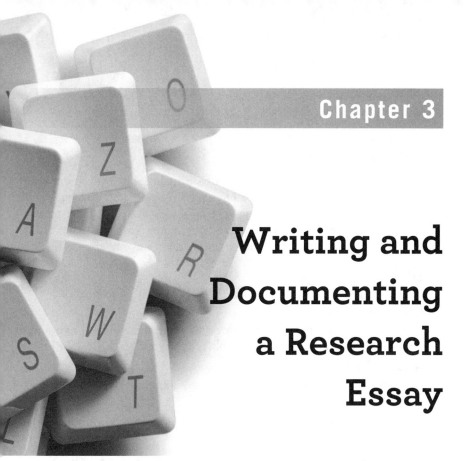

Chapter 3

Writing and Documenting a Research Essay

WRITING A BASIC RESEARCH ESSAY

In the previous sections of this guide, you learned how to get started in research, access materials, take notes, and work from a topic to a thesis and outline. Now it's time to start writing your essay. The creation of an essay is not always a linear process from brainstorming through outlining to writing; students often start part of the writing process before completely finishing the outline or thesis statement. Writing can be more like a spiral: you keep working on some sections while going back and revising others.

However, before you get too far in the writing process, go back to your outline and start filling in more details. Remember, an essay needs an introduction, thesis statement, body, and conclusion.

FROM OUTLINE TO ROUGH DRAFT

Your **introduction** probably requires the most focused writing in your essay. A good introduction serves four important purposes:

- It catches the reader's interest
- It states the topic clearly and gives background if needed
- It gives the reader an idea of how you are treating the topic
- It sets the tone and balance of the essay

Create interest by making a strong or surprising statement about your topic, engaging the sympathetic feelings of the reader, or making broad statements that then narrow to the specific topic. You may need to give some background details to familiarize your reader with the topic. Take another look at your first draft and eliminate the following errors:

Deadly:
> *In this essay, I'm going to talk about the idea of proportional representation.*

Take out the obvious ("in this essay") and the words "I'm going to." Create an interesting "hook" to get your reader's attention.

Avoid:
> *This essay is about proportional representation.*

This sentence is dull and boring. What is your point? Give a hint of what you are going to say.

Avoid:
> *There are several ideas about proportional representation that keep coming up.*

Starting an important sentence with "there is" or "there are" lacks sophistication and punch. Place your most important concept first in the sentence.

Avoid:
> *Nothing in our lifetime has been more important to Canadians than the issue of proportional representation.*

This is an exaggeration. This issue is not that important or urgent.

Avoid:
> *The characteristics of proportional representation will be discussed and readers will be informed of the benefits.*

You still have not created a clear thesis. Use active rather than passive voice and focus on the strongest point you are making.

Use instead:
Although many Canadians see proportional representation as being incompatible with parliamentary democracy, various political groups are now looking seriously at its benefits.
You should follow this statement with specific examples and your thesis statement.

The opening statement used above creates interest and introduces the topic (proportional representation debate). It also suggests the treatment (discussion of benefits) and sets the tone and balance (an analysis of benefits, with some discussion of arguments against).

The introduction of your essay should end smoothly with the **thesis statement**, which is usually found at the end of the first or second paragraph of writing. Thesis statements deserve your best work in conveying your arguments to the reader. Use clear language and good sentence structure, and avoid the pitfalls of being either too vague or too wordy.

Review the section "Choosing and Developing a Topic" in Chapter 2 and the notes on developing a topic into a thesis.

In the **body** of your essay, discuss your main points or arguments in a logical fashion (see "Organizing and Outlining Your Findings" in Chapter 2). If you have already written an outline, check to see whether your points follow one of the following types of logical order:

- Chronology
- Description or process
- Definition
- Comparison or contrast
- Classification
- Cause and effect
- Analysis/criticism

Some shorter essays might use only one of the above types of discussion. However, good analytical essays include paragraphs or short sections that use a variety of structural elements. For example, an essay on the problem of homelessness in Vancouver may explore cause and effect as well as argue for a definite solution. A research paper comparing humanitarian intervention in two different international cases might include a definition of humanitarian intervention and a chronology of events as a part of the discussion.

Connect the individual points in the body together by using transitions from one part to another. Such transition words as *first, second, moreover, in addition,* and *in conclusion* guide the reader from one point to the next. Transitions are also needed within paragraphs to organize supporting points. The body should be unified (all about the thesis) and coherent (points linked together and following a logical order).

Complete your essay by writing a strong **conclusion** that sums up your arguments. Introduce your conclusion with a good transition word that signals that these are the final thoughts of the essay. The most popular transitions to a conclusion include *in conclusion, in short, in summary,* and *finally.* Briefly summarize the main points of your essay or restate your thesis. The conclusions should state arguments in general terms and not include supporting details for any arguments. The conclusion is not the correct place to cite new information, introduce counterarguments, or leap to another topic altogether. Finally, add a concluding sentence that communicates a strong, effective message to the reader.

CHOOSING A TITLE

The title of your essay should indicate its main subject or content. Titles should be very focused—they are the first element to catch the reader's eye. A vague title that says very little or is misleading will not accomplish that purpose. Your title should describe your treatment of the subject. Some specialized assignments mentioned in Chapter 4 require specific titles or subtitles. For example, a briefing paper would include the words "A briefing paper on ___."

Avoid:
> *Human rights*
> This title is too vague. It says nothing about the content of the paper.

Avoid:
> *Human rights abuses in Syria*
> This title is also too vague. Although it identifies the country, it does not include any hint of what you are going to say on the topic.

Avoid:
> *Canadians twiddle thumbs while Syria burns*
> Do not use titles that are too wordy, informal, or sarcastic.

More focused:
> *Canada's response to human rights abuses in Syria in 2012*

TONE AND STYLE: TREAT YOUR READER WITH RESPECT

The tone and style of your essay will depend on your audience. Most writers assume that they are writing for intelligent people who have some knowledge of the topic. The tone of the essay cannot be insulting, pejorative, or too casual. Treat your readers with respect.

Examples

Wrong:
> As every intelligent person knows, torture is totally wrong.

Wrong:
> Only uninformed people would assume that some types of torture are okay.

Better:
> Many Canadians believe that any kind of torture is unacceptable.

The essay must also be readable. Using language that is either hard to understand or too casual for the audience is unprofessional. Your writing must be clear, direct, understandable, and free of gender, racial, or other biases.

Examples

Wrong: Legitimized concerns on this matter were postponed by the committee.

Better: The committee delayed discussion.

Wrong: Those guys really messed up on this one.

Better: The politicians made mistakes in their analysis.

Wrong: A cabinet minister is accountable for his decisions.

Better: Cabinet ministers are accountable for their decisions.

ESSAY CHECKLIST

When you finish your essay, go back and recheck all these points:

- ❏ Do I have a focused topic with a good thesis statement?
- ❏ Does my introduction state the thesis clearly and lead into the first points of discussion?
- ❏ Is my essay unified? Do all parts of the essay relate to the thesis?
- ❏ Have I sufficiently developed my thesis?
- ❏ Have I avoided logical fallacies?
- ❏ Are my tone and style consistent and appropriate?

❑   Have I used a variety of sentence structures and vocabulary?

❑   Have I written a strong conclusion?

❑   Have I checked for spelling errors and misused words?

❑   Have I cited all my sources in a consistent style?

❑   Have I correctly punctuated my sentences?

PROFESSIONAL PRESENTATION

The final part of the writing process is to look over every detail of your edited writing and format it in a professional way. Make your paper look polished. Pay attention to all the details of spacing, page numbering, and layout. Use a clear printer and medium-quality paper. Check the requirements for a title page. Avoid adding borders, coloured illustrations, or cartoons to the title page. A neat presentation makes a good impression on your audience.

WRITING-STYLE FAQS

1.   Why can't I use "I" (first person) in my paper?

Part of learning to write is learning what conventions or styles are expected in different situations. Academic assignments can be written in various styles. The use of first person (*I* or *we*) is appropriate for writing about personal experiences, which may occur more frequently in other disciplines, such as English or psychology. Your course assignment gives you the opportunity to learn, practice, or polish your research and writing skills. Editing out the "I" will give your work a more academic and sophisticated tone. Remember, this assignment is not about you—it's about showing your research and writing skills.

Avoid: *I found three reasons why voters in Toronto did not support using gas taxes for public transportation improvements.*

Edit out the words "I found." They are unnecessary because the audience knows the author is doing the research.

Use instead: *Voters in Toronto reported three reasons for not supporting using gas taxes for public transportation improvements.*

Now the statement is focused on the research.

2.   How can I state my opinion without writing "I think"?

Expository writing has an argument or opinion behind it. Whatever statement you make, you are going to support with facts, interpretations, and good research. A good thesis statement sets out the arguments you are making.

Avoid: *I think Canada should increase federal taxes on gasoline to save energy.*

Using plain, straightforward sentences strengthens your statements and focuses on the argument.

Use instead: *Increasing the federal tax on gasoline will save energy.*

3. *What do you mean by "audience"? Isn't my professor the only audience?*

Even though professors are the first audience for each assignment, you should approach every piece of written work with the idea that other students and teachers might read and discuss it. That concept should help you keep the tone of your writing more formal. Remember, you are practicing and polishing your writing skills. Your aim is to write in a professional manner.

4. *What's the difference between a paraphrase and a summary?*

In a paraphrase, you restate a passage using your own language. Paraphrases should be a similar length to the original passage. The idea is that you don't want to miss any ideas or details. In a summary, you restate the ideas in a passage in a more condensed form, leaving out minor points, consolidating major points, and gathering a broad range of ideas into a tight couple of sentences. Refer to the next section of this chapter for details.

5. *What is a logical fallacy?*

Research papers must provide evidence to support the main point or argument. Sometimes it is easy to find statistics but difficult to interpret those facts in such a way as to support the argument you are trying to make. *Logic* refers to the premise or reason for something and its result or conclusion. Sometimes a writer's premise and conclusion are unreasonable: that is, they do not follow sound logic.

One of the most common fallacies is known as "hasty generalization." That means that the writer is making a major assumption on the basis of one experience or on a very small body of data. If one civil servant is charged with corruption, we cannot assume that all civil servants are corrupt.

Example: Mr. Jones has been charged with accepting a bribe. Corruption in the civil service is rampant; everyone in the minister's department was accepting favours from business concerns.

For a complete listing of logical premises and fallacies, see the following websites:

The Logical Fallacies Handlist
http://web.cn.edu/kwheeler/fallacies_list.html

Stephen's Guide to the Logical Fallacies: Index
http://onegoodmove.org/fallacy/

6. My computer grammar program underlines a sentence in green and says "passive voice." What does that mean?

"Passive voice" means that the subject of the sentence does not perform the action expressed in the verb; instead, the subject receives the action. In general, the active voice is stronger and less wordy. However, you may have a good reason for using the passive voice, especially in the context of a paragraph in which the emphasis stays on a particular item.

Example: The bilateral treaty has been renewed by both countries. (passive voice)

Preferable: Both countries have renewed the bilateral treaty. (active voice)

Exception: If the writer wanted to focus the discussion on the treaty, he or she might want to leave the passive voice but eliminate the agent (by both countries).

For more information on active and passive voice, see Chapter 6.

7. What's the difference between words like lie and lay or rise and raise?

Your grammar or spell checking computer program may not tell you if you have used a word incorrectly or used the wrong word form. Many words look similar and can easily be confused. Check a list of commonly confused words and make sure you are using each word correctly. Numerous websites have lists of commonly confused words. Try http://oxforddictionaries.com/words/commonly-confused-words.

8. What should I do if I get writer's block?

Writer's block can happen to the most professional of writers. Rather than giving up entirely, it is best to keep your mind engaged with the writing task. Try working on a different section of the outline. Some ideas may come to you more easily than others. Go back to your brainstorming, review your research, and keep involved in the writing process. Don't go off on a tangent that might be a dead end. Focus on your thesis statement and the support you have already marshalled for your case. The most important thing may be scheduling enough time at the beginning of the project to allow you to deal with minor setbacks like writer's block.

9. *Why didn't I get a better mark on my assignment?*

Each instructor may have different criteria he or she is looking for when evaluating an assignment. However, instructors agree on many of the common errors that will lower your mark for your research paper:

- Careless spelling and grammatical errors
- Long quotations that don't add to the argument of the paper
- Inadequate or inaccurate citations
- Lack of a thesis statement or clear argumentation in the paper
- A paper that is off-topic or doesn't meet the requirements of the assignment
- Large fonts or extra large spacing used to pad the paper and make it look longer
- Inadequate research or evidence that the writer is unaware of common sources or arguments
- Language that is too casual for the paper
- Faulty logic, such as cause and effect, faulty premises, and unwarranted conclusions
- Charts, graphs, or illustrations that do not add to the thesis

DOCUMENTING YOUR SOURCES

INCORPORATING QUOTATIONS, PARAPHRASES, AND SUMMARIES

One of the most difficult writing tasks is incorporating quotations, paraphrases, and summaries into your paper. How many quotations should you use? How often should you paraphrase or summarize instead of quoting? What about including longer quotations? Putting together numerous quotations without much of your own analysis is not really doing a good job of analyzing the materials you have found.

Here are a few basic guidelines on using quotations, paraphrases, and summaries.

Quotations should be kept short, selected only because they state an idea in a unique way that demonstrates strong support for your thesis. Longer quotations (more than four lines or 40 words) should be used sparingly and only if the material relates strongly to the thesis statement and supports your arguments. Most students overuse both short and long quotations. Check each draft of your paper for quotations in successive paragraphs or several long quotations close together that indicate a lack of your own analysis of the content. Rethink your points of support and add your synthesis of the research. Try reworking some of the most crucial material into a paraphrase or summary. Don't forget to keep track of your sources and use citations for all quotations, paraphrases, and summaries.

All quotations, paraphrases, and summaries need to be incorporated into the text. The reader expects to find identifying information for each quote: Who said it? What are the qualifications of the person? Where was the quotation found? How does it relate to the central thesis? Quotations need to be set up, not just thrown into the middle of your analysis without explanation. Using an introductory sentence or phrase gives your reader an idea of why you have chosen the quotation.

The following is a paragraph from Jerry Z. Muller, "Us and them: The enduring power of ethnic nationalism," published in *Foreign Affairs*, Volume 87, Issue 2 (March/April 2008). We will use this paragraph to demonstrate the use of quotations in an essay:

> There are two major ways of thinking about national identity. One is that all people who live within a country's borders are part of the nation, regardless of their ethnic, racial, or religious origins. This liberal or civic nationalism is the conception with which contemporary Americans are most likely to identify. But the liberal view has competed with and often lost out to a different view, that of ethnonationalism. The core of the ethnonationalist idea is that nations are defined by a shared heritage, which usually includes a common language, a common faith, and a common ethnic ancestry.*

Examples of using material from this passage in an essay are included below in APA style.

Direct quotations are the exact words from your source. They must be enclosed in quotation marks and use correct punctuation. A parenthetical reference follows the quotation, or you can include part of the information in the introductory part of the sentence. Some quotations use an entire sentence from the source. For example:

> In his article "Us and Them," Jerry Z. Muller (2008) defines the concept of ethnonationalism: "The core of the ethnonationalist idea is that nations are defined by a shared heritage, which usually includes a common language, a common faith, and a common ethnic ancestry" (p. 20).*

The writer incorporates the author's name in the text (Jerry Z. Muller), identifies the date of publication (2008), uses correct punctuation marks, and includes the page number (p. 20) when available. The page number appears at the end following APA style. Note that the period goes *after* the parenthetical documentation, not before. This information refers the reader to the following entry in the Works Cited list:

Muller, J.Z. (2008). Us and them: The enduring power of ethnic nationalism. *Foreign Affairs*, 87(2), 18-35.

If the author's name is not mentioned in the text, the reference goes at the end of the quotation:

Nationalism has different definitions for different groups. "The core of the ethnonationalist idea is that nations are defined by a shared heritage, which usually includes a common language, a common faith, and a common ethnic ancestry" (Muller, 2008, p. 20).*

It is not necessary to use the entire sentence in the quotation. Another way to treat it is to integrate the quotation into a sentence.

According to Jerry Z. Muller (2008), ethnonationalism is a concept in which "nations are defined by a shared heritage, which usually includes a common language, a common faith, and a common ethnic ancestry" (p. 20).*

No comma is necessary before the quotation here because the quotation is blended into the grammar of the sentence. Your goal is to blend quotations into your writing and keep the parenthetical references as unobtrusive as possible.

When integrating author information into the text, use an appropriate signal phrase. This lets your reader know you are presenting the author's thoughts. Signal verbs are such words as *argues, believes, claims, concludes, defines, describes, illustrates, maintains, notes, points out, refutes, reports, says, states, suggests,* and *writes.* Use these with signal phrases as in these examples:

- As Muller (2008) notes, "This liberal or civic nationalism is the conception with which contemporary Americans are most likely to identify" (p. 20).*

- In his essay, Muller (2008) argues that the "core of the ethnonationalist idea is that nations are defined by a shared heritage, which usually includes a common language, a common faith, and a common ethnic ancestry" (p. 20).*

---

*Reprinted by permission of FOREIGN AFFAIRS, Volume 87, Issues 2, March/April 2008. Copyright 2008 by the Council on Foreign Relations, Inc. www.ForeignAffairs.com

Block quotations (more than 40 words in APA style or four lines in MLA) must be set off in a block. This means indent the entire quotation five to seven spaces from the left margin and do not use quotation marks. The page reference if necessary goes at the end in parentheses after the final period.

If you are working with documents found in databases, page numbers may not be available for documents in html format. You may need to number the paragraphs and cite by paragraph or section number where possible (para. 8).

When working with quotations, you may need to change a part of the quotation to make it fit the grammar of your sentence. For example, you might need to include a noun rather than a pronoun or show other changes for clarity. If you make any changes, brackets [ ] should be used to show what you have changed.

> Muller (2008) argues that "the liberal view [of nation-alism] has competed with and often lost out to a different view, that of ethnonationalism" (p. 20).*

If you delete part of a sentence, indicate your deletions with an ellipsis. It's not always necessary to indicate deletions at the beginning and end of a quotation. Check style guides for rules.

> As Muller (2008) states: "For substantial stretches of U.S. history, it was believed that only the people of English origin…were real Americans" (p. 20).*

As you work on your research, you may find one author who actually quotes another person. If you wish to use this as a quotation or paraphrase, you must make it clear who the original writer is and where you found the quotation. For example, in his article "The Case against a New International Environmental Organization" Adil Najam quotes Konrad von Moltke on the differences between institutions and organizations. The entire section as written by Najam is quoted here:

> The distinction, of course, is not merely semantic; it is well established in the literature and is absolutely critical to this context. Institutions, as Konrad von Moltke reminds us, are "social conventions or 'rules of the game,' in the sense that marriage is an institution, or property, markets, research, transparency or participation." Therefore, institutions need not necessarily have a physical existence (p. 368).

In using this material, be clear about who says what. For example, if you are quoting Najam, a quotation might look like this:

---

*Reprinted by permission of FOREIGN AFFAIRS, Volume 87, Issues 2, March/April 2008. Copyright 2008 by the Council on Foreign Relations, Inc. www.ForeignAffairs.com

```
Adil Najam (2003) claims that the difference between
institutions and organizations "is not merely semantic."
```

However, if you are referring to von Moltke's words, create a quotation that uses his name and a reference to the article where it was found.

```
According to Konrad von Moltke, institutions differ
because they are "social conventions" (as cited in
Najam, 2003, p. 368).
```

The work cited for both of the above quotations is entered as follows:

```
Najam, A. (2003). The case against a new international
environmental organization. Global Governance. 9(2),
367-84.
```

In this case, you do not make a separate referenced entry for von Moltke. Readers wishing to follow up on this quotation are directed to Najam's article. Check style guides for complete information.

Paraphrasing is used to restate the original ideas in your own words. Use paraphrasing to incorporate evidence into your arguments without quoting entire passages. When paraphrasing, remember these important rules:

1. Change the words. Use synonyms and restate the ideas.

2. Change the sentence structure. Rewrite the ideas in a different order.

3. Use quotation marks around strings of words taken directly without out changes.

4. Include the author's ideas without additions or deletions.

5. Start with a good signal phrase that includes author's name and date.

6. In APA style, page numbers are not required, but you can add numbers if you are paraphrasing from a longer work.

Here are three examples of paraphrases from an article by Joanna Quinn. Original quote:

```
As I define it, restorative justice is a process
of active participation in which the wider community
deliberates over past crimes, giving centre stage to
both victim and perpetrator in a process that seeks
to bestow dignity and empowerment upon victims, with
special emphasis placed upon contextual factors.
```

Paraphrase #1: The following is an example of plagiarism because it uses the author's words without quotation marks or with only slight changes.

Quinn (2010) defines restorative justice as a process of active participation. The entire community discusses past crimes with both victims and perpetrators involved in the process. They want to give dignity and empowerment to victims with special emphasis on some factors.

Paraphrase #2: The example below is also plagiarism because it attributes a different argument to the original author. In this particular quotation, Quinn does not discuss the outcome of these deliberations.

According to Joanna Quinn (2010), restorative justice focuses on both the victims and perpetrators. Groups talk about the crimes that have been committed, and these councils have worked well for everyone involved.

Paraphrase #3: The following paraphrase is both accurate and does not plagiarize the original.

Joanna Quinn (2010) argues that the process of restorative justice includes stressing the immediate circumstances at the time, involving the entire community, letting those who were persecuted and those who are guilty take part, and giving power and dignity to those who suffered from the crimes.

Summarizing refers to writing a brief overall statement of the author's argument. You must include the major ideas to be accurate, but avoid plagiarism by using quotations for longer strings of words from the original. Summaries do not include your own analysis. You are only presenting an accurate snapshot of what the original says.

Summary #1: The following example is a poor summary of Muller's paragraph listed on page 38 because it is an inaccurate interpretation of Muller's argument.

Muller (2008) argues that only the Americans think all people within their borders belong to the nation. Any other national identity, especially one based on common heritage, is not a valid definition.

Summary #2: The following summary is accurate because it follows Muller's original ideas and uses quotation marks around a word unique to Muller.

According to Jerry Z. Muller (2008), national identity can be interpreted two ways. The first way includes all people living within a country. The second interpretation is one of "enthnonationalism," or people who claim to be a nation because they share an ethnic and cultural heritage.

 Keys for using quotations, paraphrases, and summaries
- Introduce the quotation or paraphrase
- Let the reader know who the authority is
- Use only the quotations that provide a strong support for your thesis
- Make sure all quotations and paraphrases are accurate
- Keep summaries short but include all important points
- Include your own reaction, analysis, or criticism
- Use the correct punctuation and citation style

 Avoid
- Too many quotations with little of your own analysis
- Mistakes in copying quotations
- Paraphrases too close to the original
- Inaccurate summaries
- Sources used without giving credit

CITATION STYLES

This section of the guide presents examples of the three most common citation styles: APA, MLA, and Chicago. Canadian political scientists generally use the APA parenthetical notation system. However, individual instructors have their own preferences, so it is best to check the assignment instructions before submitting a final copy of your essay.

Political science research involves a great variety of sources. The examples listed here are basic ones and may not include the type of resource you need to cite. For complete listings of citation formats, consult the appropriate style manuals, online writing resources listed in Appendix I, or style sheets from your instructor or department.

AMERICAN PSYCHOLOGICAL ASSOCIATION (APA) STYLE OF CITATION

APA is referred to as the author/date system because references are alphabetized by the author's last name. The date the work was published follows the inverted name. APA style does not use quotation marks around titles. Capitalize only the first word of a title. Titles of books and larger works are italicized. Use double spacing and hanging indents.

Book with one author
Invert the author's name and use only initials instead of first and middle names. Include a space between the initials:

Chapnick, A. (2005). *The middle power project: Canada and the founding of the United Nations.* Vancouver: UBC Press.

Book with multiple authors
Invert all authors' names and use an ampersand instead of the word "and":

Weiss, T. G., Cortright, D., Lopez, G. A., & Minear, L. (1997). *Political gain and civilian pain: Humanitarian impacts of economic sanctions.* Lanham, MD: Rowman and Littlefield.

Organization as an author from web
International Accountability. (2012). Center for Economic and Social Rights. Retrieved from http://www.cesr.org

Article or chapter in an edited book
Skogstag, G. (2009). Internationalization and paradigm change: The case of agriculture. In G. Capano & M. Howlett (Eds.), *European and North American policy change: Drivers and dynamics* (pp. 91–115). New York: Routledge.

An edited collection
Carment, D., & Bercuson, D. (Eds.). (2008). *The world in Canada: Diaspora, demography, and domestic politics.* Montreal: McGill Queen's.

Two works by the same author
APA style uses the dates to determine the order of the entries, starting with the earlier date. Repeat the author's name for each entry:

Cox, R. (1987). *Production, power and world order: Social forces in the making of history.* New York, Columbia University Press.

Cox, R. (2000). Political economy and world order: Problems of power and knowledge at the turn of the millennium. In R. Stubbs and G. Underhill (Eds.), *Political economy and the changing global order* (2nd ed., pp. 25–37). Don Mills, ON: Oxford University Press.

Government publication
Elections Canada. (2011). *Survey of candidates of the 41st general election.* Retrieved from http://www.elections.ca

Article in a journal with continuous pagination

Some journals continue the page numbers throughout the entire volume. Do not include the issue number when the page numbers are continuous.

Nossal, R. K. (1982). Personal diplomacy and national behaviour: Trudeau's North-South initiatives. *Dalhousie Review, 62,* 278-291.

Article in a journal with pagination by issue number

Citations for journals that start new page numbers for each issue as below require the issue number in parentheses after the volume number.

Falkenrath, R. (2000). Weapons of mass reaction: Rogue states and weapons of mass destruction. *Harvard International Review, 22*(2), 52-56.

Internet article based on a print source

Norris, P., & Inglehart, R. (2002). Islamic culture and democracy: Testing the 'clash of civilizations' thesis [Electronic version]. *Comparative Sociology, 1,* 235-263.

Article from a database

Some databases list a DOI (digital object identifier) for each article. If a DOI is available, include it at the end of the entry. You do not need to include a retrieval date if the content is not going to change.

Chakravarty, D., & Bose, I. (2011). Industry, labour and the state: Emerging relations in the Indian state of West Bengal. *Journal of South Asian Development, 6,* 169-194. doi:10.1177/097317411100600202

Article from an e-journal

Gowan, P. (2004, Summer). Contemporary intra-core relations and world systems theory. *Journal of World-Systems Research, 10*(2). Retrieved August 30, 2004, from http://jwsr.ucr.edu/archive/vol10/number2/

Article in a newspaper without author, print

UN slams 'cruel' treatment of jailed WikiLeaks suspect. (2012, March 6). *Calgary Herald,* p. A2.

Articles from a web source

Campbell, B. (2004). False promise: Canada in the free trade era. Retrieved September 10, 2004, from the Economic Policy Institute website http://www.epinet.org/content. cfm/briefingpapers_nafta01_ca

```
CNN.  (n.d.).  The  Cold  War  experience:  Suspected  nuclear
    nations.  Retrieved  August  11,  2004,  from  http://www.cnn.
    com/SPECIALS/cold.war/kbank/maps/
```

Video file

```
Thank  you,  Kony  2012  supporters.  [Video  file].  (2012,  March
    15).  Retrieved  from  http://www.youtube.com
```

Court documents

List the plaintiff and the defendant with the court citation. Most court documents are found under the federal or provincial justice websites. For a list of terms used in Canadian court documents, see http://legalresearch. org/docs/glossary.html

```
Calgary  (City)  v.  Canada  2012  SCC  20  (2012).  Retrieved  from
    http://scc.lexum.org/en/index.html

Kwicksutaineuk/Ah-Kwa-Mish  First  Nation  v.  Canada  (Attorney
    General)  2012  BCCA  193  (2012).  Retrieved  from  http://www.
    courts.gov.bc.ca/court_of_appeal/
```

Legal documents

Legal documents require the name of the act, the *Statutes of Canada* volume and chapter numbers with a date of enactment and the website.

```
Canada  Elections  Act  SC  2000,  c.  9  (2000).  Retrieved  from
    http://www.justice.gc.ca
```

Personal interviews

Personal interviews can be a valuable source of information for researchers. If you conduct an oral interview, the source and date should be listed in the text. Do not list personal interviews in the list of references because the reader does not have access to the text. Below is an example of such an interview.

```
Although  Brian  Mason  disliked  some  aspects  of  the
    proposal,  he  supported  the  idea  of  an  all-party  com-
    mittee  (personal  communication,  April  5,  2009).
```

List of references—APA style

Below is an example of a list of references in the APA style. Note the date of publication follows the author's name. Start a separate page for the list. The entries are alphabetized by the author's last name or the title of the work if there is no author listed. Double-space the entries and use hanging indents. Consult a style manual or website for detailed information on types of sources not listed here.

References

Carment, D., & Bercuson, D. (Eds.). (2008). *The world in Canada: Diaspora, demography, and domestic politics*. Montreal: McGill Queen's.

Chakravarty, D., & Bose, I. (2011). Industry, labour and the state: Emerging relations in the Indian state of West Bengal. *Journal of South Asian Development, 6*, 169–194. doi: 10.1177/097317411100600202

Cokery, A. (2011). National human rights institutions as monitors of economic, social and cultural rights. Center for Economic and Social Rights. Retrieved from http://www.cesr.org

Cox, R. (1987). *Production, power and world order: Social forces in the making of history*. New York: Columbia University Press.

Cox, R. (2000). Political economy and world order: Problems of power and knowledge at the turn of the millennium. In R. Stubbs and G. Underhill (Eds.), *Political economy and the changing global order* (2nd ed., pp. 25–37). Don Mills, ON: Oxford University Press.

Cox, R. with Schecter, M. (2002). *The political economy of a plural world: Critical reflections on power, morals and civilisation*. Retrieved from http://www.amazon.com

Damroseh, L. F. (Ed.). (1993). *Enforcing restraint: Collective intervention in internal conflicts*. New York: Council on Foreign Relations.

Falkenrath, R. (2000). Weapons of mass reaction: Rogue states and weapons of mass destruction. *Harvard International Review, 22*(2), 52–56.

Findlay, M.H. (2010, October). The potential in a minority government. *Policy Options,* 54–55.

International Accountability. (2012). Center for Economic and Social Rights. Retrieved from http://www.cesr.org

Kwicksutaineuk/Ah-Kwa-Mish First Nation v. Canada (Attorney General) 2012 BCCA 193 (2012). Retrieved from http://www.courts.gov.bc.ca/court_of_appeal/

Riddell-Dixon, E. (2007). Canada at the United Nations in the new millennium. In D. Bratt & C. J. Kukucha (Eds.), *Readings in Canadian foreign policy: Classic debates and new ideas* (pp. 139–158). Don Mills, ON: Oxford University Press.

Scott, R. E. (2011). Growing U.S. trade deficit with China cost 2.8 million jobs between 2011 and 2010. Economic Policy Institute. Retrieved from http://www.epi.org

Soloman, L. (2012, March 9). Time for Israel to act. *Financial Post*. Retrieved from http://www.nationalpost.com

Soussan, M. (2008). *Backstabbing for beginners: My crash course in international diplomacy*. Retrieved from Ebrary Academic Complete.

Thank you, Kony 2012 supporters. [Video file]. (2012, March 15). Retrieved from http://www.youtube.com/

UN slams 'cruel' treatment of jailed WikiLeaks suspect. (2012, March 6). *Calgary Herald,* p. A2.

Weiss, T. G., Cortright, D., Lopez, G. A., & Minear, L. (1997). *Political gain and civilian pain: Humanitarian impacts of economic sanctions*. Lanham, MD: Rowman and Littlefield.

Sources to consult for APA style:

American Psychological Association. *Concise Rules of APA Style*, 6th ed. Washington, D.C.: APA, 2010.

http://owl.english.purdue.edu/owl/resource/560/05/

http://www.writing.utoronto.ca/advice/using-sources/documentation?start=2

MODERN LANGUAGE ASSOCIATION (MLA) STYLE OF CITATION

The MLA citation style is used most often in the humanities. However, your political science instructor may prefer this style. MLA differs from APA style in requirements for capitalization, use of quotation marks around titles of short works, placement of the date, inclusion of database titles, and medium of "Print" or "Web" and retrieval date at the end. Use a hanging indent and alphabetize the list by authors' last names. If there is no author, use the title of the article without counting *a*, *an*, or *the* in the title.

In-text quotations, paraphrases, and summaries must refer to both the author and page number if one is available. Readers can then easily find the original reference by author's name in the Works Cited list. Below are two examples of MLA style quotations. The first example includes the author's name in the signal phrase and a page number at the end. Do not use p. or pp. to indicate page numbers.

In his article "Us and Them," Jerry Z. Muller defines
the concept of ethnonationalism: "The core of the ethnonationalist idea is that nations are defined by a shared
heritage, which usually includes a common language, a
common faith, and a common ethnic ancestry" (20).*

If you do not include the author's name in the signal phrase, put it in parentheses at the end. Do not put a comma between author and page number.

"The core of the ethnonationalist idea is that
nations are defined by a shared heritage, which usually includes a common language, a common faith, and
a common ethnic ancestry" (Muller 20).*

Paraphrases also need author and page number at the end of the selec-
tion. Include the author's name in a signal phrase for clarity.

Joanna Quinn argues that the process of restorative
justice includes stressing the immediate circumstances
at the time, involving the entire community, letting
those who were persecuted and those who are guilty
take part, and giving power and dignity to those who
suffered from the crimes (398).

The section below contains examples of entries in MLA style and a
Works Cited list.

Book with one author, print source

Start with the author's last name, and then include the entire first name and
initial if listed. Titles of books are italicized. List only the city of publication
unless province or state is needed for clarity. Follow with the publishing
company, the year of publication, and the medium Print.

Flanagan, Thomas. *First Nations: Second Thoughts*. Montreal
and Kingston: McGill-Queen's UP, 2000. Print.

Book with multiple authors, print source

Reverse only the name of the first author. The second author remains in
normal order.

Head, Ivan, and Pierre Trudeau. *The Canadian Way: Shaping
Canada's Foreign Policy, 1968-1984*. Toronto: McClelland
and Stewart, 1995. Print.

Two works by the same author

Use a triple hyphen followed by a period to indicate repetition of the name.
In MLA style, list entries by the same author in alphabetical order by title.

*Reprinted by permission of FOREIGN AFFAIRS, Volume 87, Issues 2, March/April 2008.
Copyright 2008 by the Council on Foreign Relations, Inc. www.ForeignAffairs.com

The format (book, article, etc.) does not matter. The entries here are cited in this order because "political" comes before "production" alphabetically:

Cox, Robert. "Political Economy and World Order: Problems of Power and Knowledge at the Turn of the Millennium." Eds. R. Stubbs and G. Underhill. *Political Economy and the Changing Global Order*. 2nd ed. Don Mills, ON: Oxford UP, 2000: 25-37. Print.

---. *Production, Power and World Order: Social Forces in the Making of History*. New York, Columbia UP, 1987. Print.

An edited collection

Carment, David, and David Bercuson, eds. *The World in Canada: Diaspora, Demography, and Domestic Politics*. Montreal: McGill Queen's, 2008. Print.

Book accessed from a library database
List the database in italics and include "Web" and the access date.

Soussan, Michael. *Backstabbing for Beginners: My Crash Course in International Diplomacy*. New York: Nation Books, 2008. *Ebrary*. Web. 05 May 2012.

Article or chapter in an edited book

Skogstag, Grace. "Internationalization and Paradigm Change: The Case of Agriculture." *European and North American Policy Change: Drivers and Dynamics*. Eds. Giliberto Capano and Michael Howlett. New York: Routledge, 2009: 91-115. Print.

Article in a print journal
MLA style uses a period between the volume and issue numbers (34.3). Include the year in parentheses, but not the quarterly season (Winter, Summer). Include the page numbers.

Munton, Don, and Tom Keating. "Internationalism and the Canadian Public." *Canadian Journal of Political Science* 34.3 (2001): 517-49. Print.

Article in a journal from a library database
Include the title of the database in italics, use "Web," and list the access date.

Chace, James. "Present at the Destruction: The Death of American Internationalism." *World Policy Journal* 20.2 (2003): 1-4. *JSTOR*. Web. 06 July 2012.

Organization as author from a website

MLA does not require a web address (URL) in citations. However, if you think the reader will have difficulties finding the website, you may add the URL in angle brackets < > at the end. Some instructors may require this, so check your assignment instructions.

```
World Food Program. "WFP Anti-Fraud and Anti-Corruption
    Policy." World Food Program, 2010. Web. 06 June 2012.
```

Article from an online newspaper

```
Rinke, Andreas, and Noah Barkin. "Germany to Greece: No
    Austerity, No Aid."
nationalpost.com. National Post, 08 May 2012. Web. 10 May
    2012.
```

Online video clip

Include both the title of the website in italics and the sponsor, even if they are the same as in the example below. Insert the date on the website, the medium, and the access date.

```
"Thank You, Kony 2012 Supporters." YouTube. YouTube, 15 Mar.
    2012. Web. 06 June 2012.
```

Legal documents

Most legal documents are available online. Record the name of the act, abbreviate the *Statutes of Canada* volume and chapter numbers. Include date of enactment, source, medium, and access date.

```
Canada Elections Act. SC 2000, ch. 9. 31 May 2000. http://
    www.justice.gc.ca. Web. 04 Mar 2012.
```

Court cases

List the name of the case, the case citation information, and the year. Include the source, medium, and access date for web sources.

```
Ayangma v. French School Board 2011 PECA 3. 2011. http://
    www.gov.pc.ca. Web. 07 July 2012.
```

Personal interview

Personal interviews can be used for research. Cite the name of the person, indicate whether the interview was personal or by telephone, and include the date of the interview.

```
Labeaume, Régis. Telephone interview. 25 Sept. 2012.
```

Sample works cited list—MLA style

Below is a sample Works Cited list in MLA style. Start a new page for the Works Cited list, and centre the words "Works Cited" at the top of the page.

The entries are alphabetized by the author's last name or the title of the work if there is no author listed. All entries are double-spaced and use a hanging indent. Double-check punctuation very carefully. All MLA entries need to indicate the medium (Print or Web) and access dates for all web entries. Consult a style manual or website for detailed information on types of sources not included here.

Works Cited

Carment, David, and David Bercuson, eds. *The World in Canada: Diaspora, Demography, and Domestic Politics.* Montreal: McGill Queen's, 2008. Print.

Chace, James. "Present at the Destruction: The Death of American Internationalism." *World Policy Journal* 20.2 (2003): 1-4. *JSTOR.* Web. 06 July 2012.

Cox, Robert. "Political Economy and World Order: Problems of Power and Knowledge at the Turn of the Millennium." Eds. R. Stubbs and G. Underhill. *Political Economy and the Changing Global Order.* 2nd ed. Don Mills, ON: Oxford UP, 2000: 25-37. Print.

---. *Production, Power and World Order: Social Forces in the Making of History.* New York: Columbia UP, 1987. Print.

Flanagan, Thomas. *First Nations: Second Thoughts.* Montreal and Kingston: McGill-Queen's UP, 2000. Print.

Munton, Don, and Tom Keating. "Internationalism and the Canadian Public." *Canadian Journal of Political Science* 34.3 (2001): 517-49. Print.

Rinke, Andreas, and Noah Barkin. "Germany to Greece: No Austerity, No Aid." *nationalpost.com. National Post,* 08 May 2012. Web. 10 May 2012.

Skogstag, Grace. "Internationalization and Paradigm Change: The Case of Agriculture." *European and North American Policy Change: Drivers and Dynamics.* Eds. Giliberto Capano and Michael Howlett. New York: Routledge, 2009: 91-115. Print.

Soussan, Michael. *Backstabbing for Beginners: My Crash Course in International Diplomacy.* New York: Nation Books, 2008. *Ebrary.* Web. 05 May 2012.

World Food Program. "WFP Anti-Fraud and Anti-Corruption Policy." *World Food Program,* 2010. Web. 06 June 2012.

For more information on MLA citations, consult:

Modern Language Association. *MLA Handbook for Writers of Research Papers.* 7th ed. New York: MLA, 2009. Print.

http://writing.wisc.edu/Handbook/DocMLA.html

http://owl.english.purdue.edu/owl/resource/747/01/

THE CHICAGO MANUAL OF STYLE (CMS) STYLE OF CITATION

The Chicago Manual of Style is widely used in both history and political studies courses, and is the style required by many journal publications. CMS uses both footnotes and a bibliography at the end of the research essay. CMS bibliographic entries will include all the citations referred to in your footnotes. In some cases, notes may be placed at the end of the research work (called endnotes), followed by the bibliography. Most word processing programs include features that allow you to insert the footnote number in the text with the corresponding footnote at the bottom of the page. It's easy to edit and move footnotes without renumbering.

Both footnotes and bibliographic entries are single-spaced but double-spaced between individual entries. Start each footnote with the number, followed by a period. Single-space the entries with double spaces between. Enclose the publishing information in parentheses and use a period at the end. As with the other citation styles, alphabetize the bibliographic entries by the last name of the author and use the hanging paragraph format.

The first footnote for a work must include a full reference. Use a shortened form in subsequent references to the same author or title. Use "Ibid." alone for reference to the previous note, or "Ibid." and a page number for a consecutive note with a different page. Below are some examples of footnotes and bibliographic entries.

First footnote example:

```
1. Thomas Flanagan. First Nations? Second Thoughts. (Mon-
   treal and Kingston: McGill-Queen's, 2000), 26.
```

References to the same work later in the text use just the author's last name and a shortened version of the title with page number. In footnote #8, Ibid. tells the reader the reference is the same as footnote #7. Add a page number if needed.

```
7. Flanagan, First Nations, 43.
8. Ibid.
```

The entire entry for the same work appears in the bibliography:

```
Flanagan, Thomas. First Nations? Second Thoughts. Montreal
   and Kingston: McGill-Queen's, 2000.
```

Book with one author

1. Margaret P. Doxey, *International Sanctions in Contemporary Perspective* (New York: St. Martin's Press, 1987), 12.

Doxey, Margaret P. *International Sanctions in Contemporary Perspective*. New York: St. Martin's Press, 1987.

Book with two or three authors

2. Richard Wranghan and Dale Peterson, *Demonic Males: Apes and the Origins of Human Violence* (New York: Houghton Mifflin, 1996), 34.

Wranghan, Richard, and Dale Peterson. *Demonic Males: Apes and the Origins of Human Violence*. New York: Houghton Mifflin, 1996.

Book with an editor

3. Joy Damousi and Marilyn Lake, eds., *Gender and War* (Cambridge: Cambridge UP, 2001), 4.

Damousi, Joy, and Marilyn Lake, eds. *Gender and War*. Cambridge: Cambridge UP, 2001.

Chapter in an edited collection

4. Grace Skogstag, "Internationalization and Paradigm Change: The Case of Agriculture" in *European and North American Policy Change: Drivers and Dynamics*, eds. Giliberto Capano and Michael Howlett (New York, Routledge, 2009), 94.

Skogstag, Grace. "Internationalization and Paradigm Change: The Case of Agriculture." In *European and North American Policy Change: Drivers and Dynamics*, edited by Giliberto Capano and Michael Howlett, 91–115. New York: Routledge, 2009.

Organization as author

5. Center for Economic and Social Rights, *UN Sanctioned Suffering in Iraq* (New York: CESR, 1996), 3.

Center for Economic and Social Rights. *UN Sanctioned Suffering in Iraq*. New York: CESR, 1996.

Government publication

6. Elections Canada, *Strengthening the Foundation: Canada's Electoral System: Annex to the Report of the Chief Electoral Officer of Canada on the 35th General Election* (Ottawa: Chief Electoral Officer, 1996), 9.

Elections Canada. *Strengthening the Foundation: Canada's Electoral System: Annex to the Report of the Chief Electoral Officer of Canada on the 35th General Election.* Ottawa: Chief Electoral Officer, 1996.

Articles in print journals

7. Richard Falkenrath, "Weapons of Mass Reaction: Rogue States and Weapons of Mass Destruction," *Harvard International Review* 22, no. 2 (2000): 54.

Falkenrath, Richard. "Weapons of Mass Reaction: Rogue States and Weapons of Mass Destruction." *Harvard International Review* 22, no. 2. (2000): 52-56.

Article in a newspaper print source

8. Abdel Rahman Al-Rashed, "Terrorists Have Smeared Islam," *National Post*, September 11, 2004, A16.

Al-Rashed, Abdel Rahman. "Terrorists Have Smeared Islam," *National Post*, September 11, 2004, A16.

Article in an online newspaper

9. Andreas Rinke and Noah Barkin, "Germany to Greece: No Austerity, No Aid," *National Post*, May 8, 2012, http://nationalpost.com/.

Rinke, Andreas, and Noah Barkin. "Germany to Greece: No Austerity, No Aid." *National Post,* May 8, 2012. http://www.nationalpost.com/.

Journal article from a database

In addition to the author, title, journal title, volume, issue, and date, CMS requires the digital object identifier (DOI) if available. If there is no DOI, include the name of the database with the accession number or other identifier assigned by the database. These numbers can be found on the library database record page for each article.

10. Deepita Chakravarty and Indranil Bose, "Industry, Labour and the State: Emerging Relations in the Indian State of West Bengal," *Journal of South Asian Development,* 6, (2011): 175, doi: 10.1177/097317411100600202.

Chakravarty, Deepita, and Indranil Bose. "Industry, Labour and the State: Emerging Relations in the Indian State of West Bengal." *Journal of South Asian Development* 6, (2011): 169-194. doi: 10.1177/097317411100600202.

11. Jorge Heine and Patha Ghosh, "The Elephant in the War: India and the Afghan-Pakistan Link," *Canadian Foreign Policy,* 17, no. 1 (2011): 55, EBSCOhost (61.6845).

Heine, Jorge, and Patha Ghosh. "The Elephant in the War: India and the Afghan-Pakistan Link." *Canadian Foreign Policy* 17, no. 1 (2011): 50–61. EBSCOhost (61.6845).

Article from a website

Start with the author, title of the article, and the sponsor of the website. Access dates are not necessary: include access dates if your instructor requires them. Do not enclose URLs in angle brackets.

12. Rebecca Thiess, "The Future of Work: Trends and Challenges for Low Wage Workers," Economic Policy Institute, accessed on June 4, 2012. http://www.epi.org/publication/bp341-future-of-work/.

Theiss, Rebecca. "The Future of Work: Trends and Challenges for Low Wage Workers." Economic Policy Institute. Accessed on June 4, 2012. http://www.epi.org/publication/bp341-future-of-work/.

Online audio or video

For online sources such as postings, blogs, podcasts, and videos, include the author if available, the title of the item in quotation marks, source, date, and URL.

13. "Syrian Revolution 2012 by Algerians, Friends and Brothers," YouTube, May 10, 2012, http://www.youtube.com/watch?v=x8xL1Vsl7Vo.

"Syrian Revolution 2012 by Algerians, Friends and Brothers." YouTube. May 10, 2012. http://www.youtube.com/watch?v=x8xL1Vsl7Vo.

Government document

Legal documents require the name of the act, the *Statutes of Canada* volume and chapter numbers with a date of enactment, page number, and the URL.

14. Canada Elections Act SC 2000, c. 9 (2000), 24. http://laws-lois.justice.gc.ca/PDF/E-2.01.pdf.

Canada Elections Act SC 2000, c. 9. 2000. http://laws-lois.justice.gc.ca/PDF/E-2.01.pdf.

Court cases

15. Club Resorts, Ltd. v. Van Breda, 2012, SCC 17, (April 18, 2012), 23, Judgments of the

Supreme Court of Canada, http://scc.lexum.org/
en/2012/2012scc17/2012scc17.pdf.

Club Resorts, Ltd. v. Van Breda, 2012, SCC 17. April 18,
2012 Judgments of the Supreme Court of Canada, http://
scc.lexum.org/en/2012/2012scc17/2012scc17.pdf.

Personal interview

Personal interviews and other communications such as e-mails and telephone conversations are footnoted but not included in the bibliography.

16. Justin Trudeau, personal interview, August 25, 2012.

Sample bibliography *Chicago Manual of Style*

Bibliography

Al-Rashed, Abdel Rahman. "Terrorists Have Smeared Islam,"
National Post, September 11, 2004.

Campbell, Bruce. "False Promise: Canada in the Free Trade
Era." Economic Policy Institute. April 2001. http://www.
epinet.org/content.cfm/briefingpapers_ nafta01_ca.

Center for Economic and Social Rights. *UN Sanctioned Suffering
in Iraq*. New York: CESR, 1996.

Chakravarty, Deepita, and Indranil Bose. "Industry, Labour
and the State: Emerging Relations in the Indian State
of West Bengal." *Journal of South Asian Development* 6,
(2011): 169–194. doi:10.1177/097317411100600202.

Cox, Robert. "Political Economy and World Order: Problems of
Power and Knowledge at the Turn of the Millennium." In
Political Economy and the Changing Global Order, edited
by R. Stubbs and G. Underhill, 2nd ed., 25–37. Don Mills,
Ontario: Oxford University Press, 2000.

———. *Production, Power and World Order: Social Forces in the
Making of History*. New York: Columbia University Press,
1987.

Damroseh, Lori Fisler, ed. *Enforcing Restraint: Collective
Intervention in Internal Conflicts*. New York: Council on
Foreign Relations, 1993.

Doxey, Margaret P. *International Sanctions in Contemporary
Perspective*. New York: St. Martin's Press, 1987.

Falkenrath, Richard. "Weapons of Mass Reaction: Rogue States
and Weapons of Mass Destruction." *Harvard International
Review* 22, no. 2 (2000): 52–56.

Nossal, Richard Kim. "Personal Diplomacy and National Behaviour: Trudeau's North-South Initiatives." *Dalhousie Review* 62 (1982): 278-91.

"Syrian Revolution 2012 by Algerians, Friends and Brothers." YouTube. May 10, 2012. http://www.youtube.com/watch?v=x8xL1Vsl7Vo.

Weiss, Thomas G., et al. *Political Gain and Civilian Pain: Humanitarian Impacts of Economic Sanctions.* Lanham, MD: Rowman and Littlefield, 1997.

For more information on CMS, see

http://www.chicagomanualofstyle.org/home.html

http://owl.english.purdue.edu/owl/resource/717/04/

http://polisci.washcoll.edu/citationguides.php

MISTAKES AND SOLUTIONS

Use your paper as a learning experience. If you receive a low mark, talk to your instructor and find out why. Here are some of the most common problems that appear in students' papers along with solutions you can use in your next assignment.

Problem	Solution
Incomplete or inconsistent documentation	Take careful bibliographic notes using the suggestions in "Developing a Working Bibliography" in Chapter 2. Proofread carefully to ensure consistency. Review the style sheets or websites for the requirements.
Too many quotations or bad use of quotations in the text	Revise your drafts to include only those quotations that really pack a punch and get the reader's attention. Work at paraphrasing and adding more of your own analysis. See the section in this chapter on using quotations.

Problem	Solution
Plagiarism	Educational institutions have serious penalties for plagiarism. You need more practice in paraphrasing, summarizing, and amalgamating ideas using your own words.
Mechanics—spelling, grammar, and punctuation errors	Carefully edit and proofread to eliminate most errors. Have another person read over your material—your tutor, friend, writing specialist. Refer to Chapter 6 for grammar, mechanics, and websites for help.
Style—too informal; simplistic writing without sentence variety; or a fake intellectual tone (big words but unclear writing)	Check websites for more information on writing style.
Weak thesis; lack of support for thesis statement; thesis does not fit content of paper	Go back to the brainstorming and organizing parts of your paper. Make sure every paragraph forms some element of support for the thesis.
Inadequate research; too few resources; reliance on one major source rather than a variety of sources	Spend more time researching and organizing your findings. Research a number of sources, even if you don't use them all in your Works Cited list. Look for books, scholarly journals, and reputable websites. Get assistance for library research in databases. Learn how to evaluate primary and secondary sources.
Lack of organization or logical development of the argument	Review the different types of essays and revise your outline. Check each section for the keys to clarify how to organize the essay.

(Continued)

Problem	Solution
Arguments contain logical fallacies that invalidate thesis	Review the various kinds of logical fallacies. Do more work at the research stage to get a well-balanced view of the problem.
Requirements of the assignment not fulfilled	Make sure you understand the assignment. Discuss the requirements with your instructor or tutor. Ask if you can submit an outline for approval before proceeding to the writing phase. Check the website for Using English for Academic Purposes: A Guide for Students in Higher Education at http://www.uefap.co.uk.
Good ideas but writing is hard to follow	Work on adding transitions, both within paragraphs and between major sections of the paper. Make sure your introduction and thesis statement give the reader an idea of how you will develop your thesis. Develop coherence in your writing.

Remember: The biggest problem students have is not allowing enough time to do a thorough job on each step of the assignment.

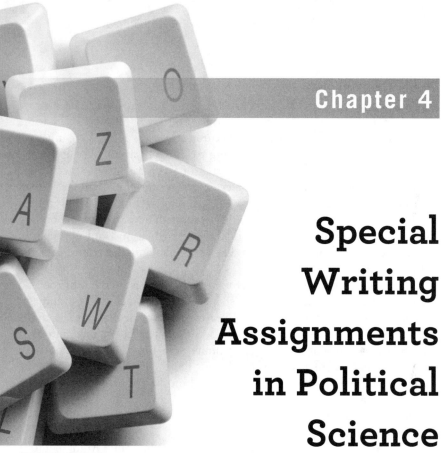

© malerapaso/iStockphoto

Chapter 4

Special Writing Assignments in Political Science

ARGUMENTATIVE WRITING AND ISSUE REACTION PAPERS

Some political science writing assignments, such as issue reaction papers and op-ed articles, require strong argumentative writing. This means that the writer is trying to persuade the readers to change their minds and support a different point of view on a specific question. Argumentative writing is different from general expository writing because argumentative writing contains a strongly stated thesis that is usually emotive—that is, it stirs up the emotions of the reader. The writer wants to change opinions or inspire action on an issue.

Successful argumentation requires a strong thesis statement that reveals the author's opinion, some support or evidence for the proposed theory, and a thorough knowledge of the opposing arguments. You must follow several guidelines when writing with an argumentative purpose.

DEFINE THE ARGUMENT

It is easy to point out that there are two sides to every discussion; however, it is much more difficult to define your own opinion on a topic and write about it in a clearly structured manner. First, you must be certain that there is, in fact, something to disagree about. For example, the United Nations has been an international organization since 1945. No one can dispute that fact. However, if a writer says that the United Nations has been totally ineffective in preventing human rights abuses inside a country, many people would disagree. The writer is responding to the issue of the ineffectiveness of the United Nations and is prepared to present the arguments in such a way as to persuade the reader to agree with the thesis.

Second, an argumentative essay is more than a restatement of the two sides of the question. If you only list facts in both sides of an argument, you do not give your audience any idea of how you feel about the topic. Remember, an argumentative essay does more than just organize information; it uses persuasion to change opinions on a topic. An argumentative essay takes one side of a controversial issue; there should be no doubt in the reader's mind where you as the writer stand on that issue.

Arguments have to be manageable for the scope of the work assigned. You are responding to a particular question or issue. For example, a two-page essay on the topic of abolishing the United Nations would not begin to cover the relevant arguments and evidence on the topic. Argumentative writing is focused on a particular, well-defined issue or question.

INVESTIGATE THE OPPOSITION

To be convincing, you have to both find strong support for your own arguments and have a thorough knowledge of the opposing side. When researching the arguments, anticipate opposing viewpoints and be ready to refute them in the essay. Casting doubt on another's position or reasoning can be done in several ways:

- Cite authorities that hold the opposing view and then use your own research to refute their arguments.
- Construct your rebuttal by mentioning personal experiences or anecdotal information that creates a different picture.
- Attack the opposition's interpretation of documents and facts.

Writers often concede some of the arguments that an opponent makes and then challenge the opponent with a strong conclusion. Concessions should be included early in the essay. Your strongest points should be left to the end, leaving no doubt in the reader's mind of your intentions. Avoiding any mention of the opposing position is not a good strategy.

When building support for your own conclusion, be careful to avoid argumentative fallacies or mistakes in reasoning. If you do not thoroughly examine the causes of homelessness, for example, you might end up making an incorrect statement like "All homeless people have a mental illness." Careful research and analysis are necessary to avoid making crucial mistakes in reasoning. Several of the websites listed in Appendix I contain detailed information on logical fallacies.

ISSUE REACTION PAPERS

One type of assignment that requires an argumentative approach is an issue reaction paper. Issue reaction papers (also called issue response papers) are intended to be controversial. In defending one side of a controversial topic, you will gain practice in analyzing and criticizing all the arguments on both sides of an issue. For example, if you are working on the topic of capital punishment, the controversial statement for the assignment might be "Capital punishment should be reinstated." To present an effective argument on either the yes or the no side, you have to familiarize yourself with analyses, research, and criticisms of both points of view. For this reason, issue reaction papers are a good way to prepare for a debate on the assigned topic. Like other essays and assignments, an issue reaction paper requires thorough research and a well-crafted thesis statement that is supported by evidence. In addition, an issue reaction paper must include a refutation of the opposition's major points and a strongly worded concluding paragraph.

The first step in writing an issue reaction is to decide what question or statement you are responding to. Your instructor may give out the general topic and let you decide which way to react. An issue might be "Canada's military presence in the polar region." We know this statement has two sides: those who think we need a stronger presence and those who feel a larger military presence would be too costly. You choose which side you are on and create the thesis statement.

Other assignments may have a previously determined issue, and you will react with a yes or no. For example, questions in textbooks or readers may take opposing sides to a particular question, such as "Do we need an international criminal court?"

All issue reaction papers begin with an attention-getter; you can quote an interesting fact, make a dramatic statement, or even quote the opposite opinion. An opening statement for a paper in favour of an international criminal court, for example, might begin with "Most dictators in the past 100 years have never been punished for their crimes." Of course, the rest of the paper would include evidence of this argument. The point is that your opening statement has caught the attention of the reader.

Another important requirement in an issue reaction paper is to define the problem. Why is there a problem with international figures committing crimes against humanity? What is the role of an international court of justice? How effective has it been in curbing crimes against humanity? Brainstorming will help you identify the most important questions surrounding the issue.

Issue reaction papers also contain concessions and refutations. A concession is your admission that part of your opponent's arguments might be correct. However, you concede only the minimum and go on to show how your opponent is incorrect on other points. Using a concession is an argumentative device that helps you persuade the audience to your opinion. On the topic of homelessness, you might concede that "although we both agree that the number of homeless people in Vancouver is too high, your solution of subsidized housing will not work."

The structure of an issue reaction paper can take two forms:

PATTERN I

Introduction
Thesis statement
Background of the issue—defining the problem
Arguments with supporting evidence
Refutation of all your opponent's points
Reminder of your strongest arguments
Conclusion, including a strong opinion statement

PATTERN II

Introduction
Thesis statement
Background information—defining the problem
Statement of your opponent's first argument, with refutation
Statement of your opponent's second argument, with refutation
Continued refutation of your opponent's arguments, in order
Conclusion, with a strong statement of your opinion

Pattern I is better for shorter papers in which it is fairly easy to follow the arguments and fewer points of supporting evidence are used. Longer reaction papers would follow Pattern II, because it is easier to include more details or longer analyses of evidence without the reader losing track of the arguments. In both cases, your conclusion needs to be strong. Leave the reader with a strong impression of your arguments.

Keys to a good issue reaction
- Clearly define the issue
- Take a strong position
- Back up your position with evidence from a variety of sources
- Defend your position by defusing the opposition
- Make a strong conclusion

 Avoid
- Making or being led into logical fallacies
- Getting off-topic
- Using suspect, unreliable, or outdated information for support
- Attacking the person (opposition supporter) rather than the information

For examples of issue reaction writing, see the following works:

- Benson, I. T. (2013). Living together with disagreement: Pluralism, the secular, and the fair treatment of beliefs in Canada today. In M. Charlton & P. Barker. (Eds.), *Crosscurrents: Contemporary political issues*. (7th ed.). Toronto: Thomson Nelson.
- Miljan, L. (2013). Political bias in the media. In M. Charlton & P. Barker. (Eds.), *Crosscurrents: Contemporary political issues* (7th ed.). Toronto: Thomson Nelson.

POLICY ANALYSIS PAPER

The purpose of a policy analysis paper is to assist decision-makers in formulating or improving policies. Policy analysis papers are used at all levels of government, by business and charitable groups, and for educational institutions. Some policy analysis papers are written by individuals, but often a team will collaborate to ensure comprehensive research and analysis. Policy analysis papers deal with finding solutions to current problems and are not intended to be theoretical or overly general in nature. Instead, they have the very practical objective of identifying and evaluating the policy options for a specific "real-world" topic or problem.

Theoretically oriented papers in political science may deal with a broad question, such as "Is globalization undermining the power of the state?" Here, the writer explores the concepts of globalization and the state from a theoretical viewpoint and examines arguments relating to the impact of globalization on the powers of the state. The purpose of such a paper is to advance the overall understanding of the concepts of globalization and the state, and to add to current theories of the relationship between the two.

In contrast, a policy analysis paper focuses on a particular problem posed by globalization for state policymakers; for example, what can policymakers do about the domestic job losses in the face of a globalizing economy? In this case, the author identifies why the issue of domestic job loss is a problem and then examines possible alternative courses of action available to policymakers.

Effective policy papers follow an organizational pattern that leads the reader through the various elements of definition, background, alternatives, and conclusions. An outline for a basic policy paper should have these points in order:

- Problem definition
- Background and policy context
- Policy alternatives
- Evaluation of policy alternatives
- Recommendations and implementation
- References

In addition, policy papers written for advanced courses or in a professional setting may require an executive summary, a table of contents, and appendices for additional information.

For each section of the policy paper, you need to consider a number of issues and questions. Under the section of **problem definition**, readers expect to find the following:

- A description of the current situation or issue that is to be addressed
- A discussion on why the current policy is a problem
- Research on current policies and an explanation of why they are inadequate
- A listing of other policies that may have an impact on this issue, either negatively or positively
- A discussion of what goals or objectives should be addressed in resolving the issue
- Criteria to measure the success of a new policy

It is important to clearly define the current situation. Your audience has to know from the outset what particular point you will be addressing in the paper.

For example, you may be assigned to write a policy paper addressing policy responses to the issue of prostitution. How you define the nature of the "problem" will be crucial to the rest of the essay. You might focus on one particular type of prostitution, such as street walking. In this case, you may focus on prostitution as a social evil that degrades the quality of life in a community; therefore, a successful policy to address prostitution would be measured by the absence of prostitution from a particular neighbourhood.

Another student may look at the problem of street prostitution from the perspective of the sex trade workers. The definition of the problem would then encompass the issues of the health and safety of sex trade workers. Criteria to measure the success of a new policy might focus on the protection of sex trade workers' rights to earn an income in a safe environment. Clearly, depending on which way you define the issue, the list of policy alternatives will be quite different.

The second part of your discussion is the **background and policy context**. It provides information on the background, evolution, and current state of the issue. Policies are generated because of needs; policies develop in the context of a specific set of circumstances that may both shape the choices that are made and limit their success. A good policy context should take into account political, social, and economic factors that have contributed to the emergence of the issue as a problem in public policy.

Another factor in the policy context is explaining what parts of a current policy work and what parts are ineffective. In effect, you are breaking down a policy into individual elements and evaluating each part. If your audience is going to agree with policy changes, it needs to know what the problems are with the current policy. Your rationale for change is based on the analysis of the current situation.

The third section of your paper will discuss **policy alternatives**. This section must be clearly structured, discussing each alternative in turn. Most authors divide the discussion into numbered or titled sections. You are writing a descriptive list of various options to solve a problem. Each option may have its own list of steps to be taken, and the options should provide a comprehensive response and not depend on other options for implementation.

After you have listed all the options, you conduct an **evaluation of policy alternatives**. A complete analysis of policy alternatives considers some or all of the following factors:

- Social and economic benefits for primary and secondary groups
- Possible negative impacts on primary and secondary groups
- Costs of implementation
- Length and stages of the implementation process
- Length of time this policy would be valid (would it have to be changed in x number of years?)

For example, a municipal government may be evaluating its current policy of banning secondary suites in single-family homes. Its options might include allowing anyone to construct suites, allowing suites in limited areas, giving incentives for more low-cost rental housing, or keeping the status quo. The primary groups would be renters and homeowners. Secondary groups might be the local schools (the changes would affect student enrolment) and city services (increases in water usage, amounts of garbage, inspection of suites, property taxes). Costs and benefits will vary with each option, as will the length and stages of implementation. The length of time the policy would be valid might vary depending on demographic shifts or housing costs for the average family.

When you are evaluating the various options, structure the discussion for each option in the same way; this arrangement makes it easier for the reader to compare the points in the discussion. Do not make suggestions for alternatives that are impossible to fulfill. For example, finding ways to address the problem of low-cost rental accommodation would not include building an apartment block when no money is available for that option.

Some policy analysis studies look at costs and benefits from a social or political point of view. The social costs of implementing a new policy might be balanced against the social or political benefits. Cost-benefit analysis is a very specialized field, especially when determining monetary costs. In a team project, a qualified financial analyst may assist in calculating the actual monetary costs and benefits. It is important to give a clear and objective accounting of all anticipated costs and benefits. Ignoring potential costs or benefits in order to make another alternative look better may only serve to discredit your analysis.

In working on a course assignment, you may need to rely on available data to support your various policy alternatives. For example, an assignment to analyze various benefits of the current immigration policy might use data from Statistics Canada on employment levels among recent immigrants.

Perhaps the most important section of a policy analysis discusses the **recommendations and implementation.** The ultimate purpose of policy analysis is to recommend which alternative would be the best. The discussion may include a summary of the cost-benefit analysis and an explanation of why a particular alternative was selected. However, as seasoned policymakers are quick to point out, just making a decision does not resolve a problem. A policy must be implemented, and it is often at this stage that the best-intended policies come to ruin. In putting forward a preferred policy solution, point out any particular considerations that would have a negative impact on policy implementation.

All the information used in a policy analysis paper should be carefully cited and thoroughly documented. Many published documents have a formal style of footnotes or endnotes using *The Chicago Manual of Style*. However, for course assignments, your instructor may require or permit parenthetical references.

After the paper is completed, you should write a one- to two-page **executive summary** to be placed at the beginning of the report. An executive summary sets out the basic issue being addressed, the alternatives being reviewed, and a brief statement of the concluding recommendations.

A good executive summary serves several purposes. It condenses information for quick reading. It also focuses the arguments so that researchers know at a glance whether to continue reading, and it ensures that your main points are given due attention and not overlooked in a long document. Executive summaries are often listed in other resource works to guide researchers and policymakers.

A policy analysis paper must walk a fine line between providing sufficient information to make a reasoned and intelligent decision, and not overwhelming the reader with too much detail and minutiae. Policymakers are often pressed for time and face large amounts of documentation. **Appendices** allow you to provide supporting information without getting bogged down in too much detail. Maps, graphics, diagrams, and tables summarizing statistical material are appropriate materials to add in the appendices, if you feel the reader needs this information to make a sound judgment. In most cases, you would not include other articles or government reports that you have cited. You should note them with a citation in the bibliography.

 Keys to a good policy paper

- Concisely define the problem or issue
- Analyze all the factors
- Fairly consider all the alternatives
- Make strong recommendations for a course of action

 Avoid

- Suggesting impossible solutions
- Excluding information on one option because you do not favour it
- Using faulty logic in cause and effect
- Exaggerating the benefits or underestimating the real costs
- Padding the appendices with marginal information

For more information on how to do policy analysis, see "Steps for a Successful Policy Analysis" at the following website: http://www.socialresearchmethods.net/kb/analysis.php

Policy analysis often involves the use of precise measures of costs and benefits. Some useful tools in conducting cost-benefit analyses are found at the following website:

http://www2.sjsu.edu/faculty/watkins/cba.htm

Various government and advocacy organizations publish policy analysis reviews on their websites. For examples of federal documents on policy research, see the following websites:

Policy Horizons Canada

http://www.horizons.gc.ca/page.asp?pagenm=pub_index

For examples of public policy papers, see:

The North-South Institute

http://www.nsi-ins.ca/pages/policy_briefs.html

The Institute for Research on Public Policy

http://www.irpp.org/cpa/index.php

For print resources on the skills and techniques of policy analysis, see the following:

- Dunn, W. N. (2012). *Public policy analysis: An introduction* (5th ed.). Upper Saddle River, NJ: Pearson/Prentice Hall.
- Wheelan, C. (2011). *Introduction to public policy.* NY: W.W. Norton.

BRIEFING PAPERS

A briefing paper is probably one of the most common forms of writing for those working in the public policy domain. A briefing paper provides an official or a group with an accurate and comprehensive outline of a particular problem or issue. It identifies the most important and contentious issues and critically assesses the implications. To be effective, briefing papers must be succinct and well organized.

Government agencies produce briefing papers to satisfy the needs of a particular official or committee. Lobby or special interest groups also put forth briefing papers to inform both government officials and the general public of their proposed solution to a problem. Here are a few typical examples of situations when briefing papers are commonly used:

- The Minister of International Trade is scheduled to attend a meeting with his or her counterpart in Washington, D.C., and needs to know what the outstanding trade issues are in Canadian–American relations.

- A busy Member of Parliament cannot attend some local environmental hearings regarding a controversial project in her riding, so she sends a junior staff member to write a summary of the issues raised in the hearing.

- In anticipation of an upcoming United Nations Conference on global hunger, a research institute wants to apprise both governmental policymakers and informed members of the public about the importance and significance of the issues likely to be addressed at the conference.

- In response to the announcement of a government policy or to unfolding events, an advocacy group wants to publicize its own perspective on the issues. In such circumstances, the briefing paper may take on more the quality of a position paper, since it may want to give the reader the background necessary not only to understand a public issue but also to ensure that the position adopted by the group is known.

Briefing papers assume a more informed audience and usually serve informational purposes. Unlike argumentative pieces, briefing papers do not need to grab the reader's attention or to provoke human interest. The reader will want to grasp a complete and comprehensive understanding of a complex issue in as brief and concise a form as possible. The challenge is to keep the document brief but not to oversimplify the issue so much that your presentation is inadequate or misleading.

In writing a briefing paper, it is important that you include only what the reader needs to know to respond intelligently to the issue. The material must be presented in a format that can be easily digested in a very short time. Unlike a longer research paper, briefing papers contain more heads, subheads, and bulleted points. It must be easy to skim the document to find the most important points.

ORGANIZING A BRIEFING PAPER

Most briefing papers are divided into three parts:

- An introduction that states the issue and its current importance
- The background and context of the issue
- The outlook or implications of the issue

Introduction

The first paragraph of the introduction establishes the focus and scope of the paper. You do not need to include the essay conventions of a hook, interest building, or a thesis statement. Instead, your briefing paper will clearly state the issue and the reasons for developing a briefing paper. Some of those reasons may include the following:

- Current events that require a response or position statement. These could include a news conference, press interview, or question period in Parliament.
- Upcoming negotiations or conferences at which a position must be defended.
- The need for immediate action to avert a crisis.
- A summary of actions taken by a group or organization in response to an issue.

The introduction should briefly state the importance of the issue and the time limit on its importance. It should also introduce the issues at stake. Some briefing papers focus largely on the nature of the issue and contending approaches to it. Others look at the various parties involved and their individual interests and positions on the issue.

Background and Context

The main body of the briefing paper presents a more detailed analysis of the topic. What this section includes is determined both by the nature of the issue and by the needs of the reader. In some cases, the paper will focus more on alternative concepts or approaches to the problem. In other cases, it may focus more on the participants in the debate and their stakes in the outcome.

For example, in the briefing paper "Right to Water: Legal Forms, Political Channels," the writers focus on the notion that responses to the problem of ensuring access to water can be based on three different approaches: human rights, contractual rights, and property rights. An alternative analysis would examine who the different participants are, identify their interests or stake in the water access issue, and analyze the positions that they have taken. The discussion could include the positions taken by industrial nations versus developing countries, the views of land-locked countries as opposed to coastal nations, or statements from development organizations compared with those from multinational corporations.

A writer of a briefing paper must ensure that he or she has included all major factors. Most briefing papers are kept in an easy-to-read format by using headings for individual sections and bulleted lists where appropriate. It's important to keep the briefing information within the specified limits requested. Writing a five-page briefing for an official who will only read the first two pages is unproductive.

Outlook and Implications

Normally, briefing papers are primarily a summary of an issue without much additional comment or analysis. However, some papers are prepared by senior officials or by a researcher with expertise in the field; in such cases, the briefing paper would probably include additional analysis and comment. Comments and recommendations might include the following:

- Developments that may complicate resolution of the issue
- The implications of the proposed outcomes
- More information that needs to be gathered before the issues can be resolved
- A possible course of action

Briefing papers are objective and neutral in tone. You want to convey to the reader the main issues under discussion, show where the divisions of opinion or disagreements are, and provide some analysis of the implications of the outcome. Making recommendations depends on the audience for the paper. Decision-makers will want to draw their own conclusions. However, if you are writing a briefing paper to inform the public of an issue, you may want to suggest a solution or course of action. If you compare the briefing papers listed below, you will see that some are informational, while others make fairly strong recommendations for change.

A good example of an informational briefing paper issued by an independent research institute is the "Brief Presented to the UN Special Rapporteur on the Right to Food" compiled by the Canadian Centre for Policy Alternatives, 2012. It is available at http://www.policyalternatives.ca. This briefing paper consists of listing changes in government policies and current statistics on poverty and the working poor in Canada.

Kairos Canada has published a number of briefing papers and policy statements that make recommendations for change. For example, see "Policy Briefing Paper #30, Coal and Shale Gas: Obstacles to Climate Justice" (2011), which is available at http://www.kairoscanada.org. Many online briefing papers contain links to other organizations and research documents on the same topic.

Citations

Briefing papers commonly refer to other writers and documents. To keep the focus on the text, it is best to use footnotes or endnotes and add an accompanying bibliography for full citations. Other documentation of interest can be included in appendices, if necessary. Because many briefing papers appear on the Web as public information, they may also include links to other websites for more information.

 Keys to a briefing paper

- Include a brief and concise summary
- Present the information in easy-to-read format
- Ensure the accuracy of your information

 Avoid

- Oversimplifying the issue
- Writing long paragraphs
- Including irrelevant facts or off-topic information

For other examples of briefing papers, see the following websites:

Overseas Development Institute

http://www.odi.org.uk

United Nations High Commission on Refugees

http://www.unhcr.org

CRITICAL REVIEWS

You have probably read critical review articles in newspapers or even heard critics on TV review books, films, or plays. A critical review paper in political science is similar to these more popular forms in that it presents a critical analysis of a work based on knowledge of the field. To write a good critical review of a book or journal article, you need in-depth knowledge of the subject area.

Critical reviews begin with a citation of the author and work before the first paragraph. This information allows the reader to quickly identify the author and book or journal. For example, if you are writing a review of Robin Craig's book *Comparative Ocean Governance*, you must put the complete bibliographic information at the top of the page. Use the required citation style (APA, MLA, or CMS) or follow this template: title, author, place of publication, publisher, date, and number of pages.

Comparative Ocean Governance: Place-Based Protections in an Era of Climate Change. Robin K. Craig. Northampton, MA: Edward Elgar, 2012. 200pp.

The first paragraph should contain more information about the author and the work, written in a "hook" format to get the reader's interest. Like all good expository writing, a critical review contains a thesis statement, reflecting your analysis of the work.

The body of the review will contain an overview of the contents, a presentation of the main ideas, and your analysis of the work. Many students make the mistake of writing a long summary of the work, with only a few sentences of analysis at the end. The overview of the contents should be as brief as possible yet inform the reader of the major themes and ideas presented. The focus should be on the main arguments presented in the work and your critique of them.

An outline of the review can take two different forms, depending on the length of your review. For shorter reviews, the following paragraph organization is preferred:

I. Introduction

II. Body

   A. Overview of the work

   B. Author's main arguments

   C. Criticism and analysis

   D. Comments on the value of the work

III. Conclusion

For longer reviews, deal with each argument before proceeding to the next one. Your outline will look more like this:

I. Introduction

II. Body

   A. Overview of the work

   B. Author's first point with your analysis

   C. Author's second point with your analysis

   D. Author's third point with your analysis

III. Comments on the value of the work

IV. Conclusion

The main challenge of writing a critical review article is keeping the focus on an **analysis of the author's views,** not a presentation of your own opinions of the subject. You may have biases up front, which you may mention briefly in the introduction, but your ideas are not the focus of the article. For example, you may be an ardent economic nationalist reviewing a book defending free trade. It may be helpful for the reader to know that you come with an anti–free trade bias, but the purpose is not to discuss and explain your own views of the subject. Rather, you want to show that the author has not made a convincing case. You might simply want to highlight ideas that have caused you to rethink your position.

To write a thorough and fair review, you need to be knowledgeable in the field you are writing about. Broad study in the area will help you answer the following questions when assessing the worth of the book or article:

- What contribution does the book/article make to the study of politics?
- How does the work compare with other works in the field?
- What is new or original with this work?
- Does it make new information available?
- Does it provide an alternative interpretation of the topic?
- How thorough is the author in presenting the research?
- What are the strengths and weaknesses of the book/article?
- How will reading the book/article benefit the reader of your review?

A good review will place a book/article in the context of the subject being studied and the literature that may already exist. For example, suppose you wanted to review *The End of Growth* by Jeff Rubin. You would need to explain the context of the debt crisis in Europe, rising oil prices, and the slowing growth rate of economies around the world. Include biographic information about the author that may be important. In this case, Jeff Rubin is a former economist who has written other books on the economy.

You may need to place the book/article in the context of what other reviewers have said. Perhaps you disagree with another reviewer's critical analysis, or you feel that the author's contribution has been misunderstood and needs to be reevaluated.

A critical review is not synonymous with criticism in a negative manner. Critical reviews can contain both positive and negative comments. If you think the author has done an excellent job, you should be prepared to give credit for it. Your assessment must also take into consideration the objectives of the book and critically assess whether the author has convincingly achieved them. You cannot criticize authors for not writing what was not intended. For example, you would not criticize this guide as being inappropriate for history students when it is not intended for that group.

To write a good critical review, it is useful to read some reviews of other political science books. Many political science journals, like the

Canadian Journal of Political Science, have extensive book review sections. Also, many journals specialize in providing reviews of notable books, often written by other specialists in the field. Check out *The New York Times Review of Books, The Times Literary Supplement,* or the book section that is a regular feature of the Saturday *Globe and Mail.*

 Keys to a critical review

- Identify the author and the work
- Include a brief but accurate summary
- Complete a thorough analysis of the main arguments
- Write a statement of the contribution this work has made
- Provide strong support for your praise and criticisms

 Avoid

- Writing a summary that is too long, with little or no analysis
- Using repetitive starts to sentences and paragraphs (the author says, she states, she writes; Chapter One is about, Chapter Two is about)
- Providing weak or insufficient support for your analysis
- Including vague comments or too personal comments (I liked, I enjoyed, I think)

For more on writing general book reviews, see the following websites:

http://library.queensu.ca/inforef/bookreview/write_review.htm

http://www.library.mun.ca/guides/howto/write_book_review.php

 **OP-ED ARTICLES**

WHAT IS AN OP-ED ARTICLE?

Op-eds are articles submitted to newspapers to express an opinion about a particular public issue. Op-ed articles give an opportunity for expressions of opinion that may differ from the official editorial stance taken by a newspaper. The term "op-ed" derives from "opposite the editorial page" since they have traditionally been placed in the newspaper on the page opposite to official editorials written by newspaper staff. Their placement suggests that they offer an "opinion" or a particular analysis of an issue rather than the "hard news" in the rest of the paper.

Although op-ed articles give the "private citizen" an opportunity to contribute to public debate on an issue, they differ from "letters to the editor." Letters to the editor are limited in length and may express a strong opinion or reaction to a particular news item. Most letters are submitted by the public, although some may be from a particular group or organization.

In contrast, op-ed pieces are generally longer and give a more careful and reasoned analysis of an issue, showing why opposing viewpoints are wrong or misguided. Writers who have specialized experience in or knowledge of an issue have an opportunity to express their own unique perspective. Thus, writers of op-ed articles are often community activists, university professors, researchers, politicians, lawyers, or business leaders. In addition, syndicated columnists who specialize in certain areas of public policy regularly contribute op-ed articles to major newspapers. For example, syndicated columnists Lysiane Gagnon, Margaret Wente, and Andrew Coyne have contributed to public policy debates on a variety of issues. Some university professors, such as William Watson from McGill University and David Bercuson from the University of Calgary, regularly write op-ed articles in national newspapers.

The writing style of an op-ed article is unique compared with the other styles of political science writing; it must both appeal to a broad audience and show depth of research and analysis. Op-ed writing cannot be an impersonal reporting of facts or theories. Rather than just presenting factual analysis and data, an op-ed piece uses persuasive argumentation to provide a more dramatic picture of the human impact of public policy issues.

FORMAT FOR OP-ED ARTICLES

Introduction

Successful op-ed articles must get the reader's attention and clearly express the writer's point of view at the outset. After reading the opening paragraph, the reader should know exactly what the writer's position on this issue is. The opening paragraph conveys why the issue is important and builds emotional ties to the reader. The writer also states his or her qualifications to write about this topic. For example, a writer who has just returned from a field visit to the Middle East will use personal experiences to connect with readers when writing about violence and human rights abuses in Syria.

Body

Op-ed pieces have a number of purposes. They not only show why opposing viewpoints are incorrect, but they also create an emotional connection to influence readers to agreement and possibly action. To accomplish this dual purpose, the body of the op-ed article must support the introductory and thesis statements with strong evidence written in audience-friendly language.

In some cases, you can provide data or statistics that have been overlooked or ignored in previous debates. You may want to provide an alternative interpretation of recently released data. For example, someone writing on crime might report on a recent increase in the crime rate but interpret the data to show that there is no need for public alarm.

Another way to provide evidence is to quote various experts in the field. Show your knowledge of the subject matter by citing reliable experts. A final way to create support for your argument is personal or anecdotal evidence. For example, a provincial government states that it is possible to live on a social assistance allowance of $500 per month, but you have anecdotes from people who have tried it and can tell about the difficulties.

Writers of op-ed pieces need to give strong, descriptive examples that emphasize the human dimensions of an issue. Check your vocabulary and expressions to see whether you have chosen a variety of words that will build an image in the reader's mind.

In making your arguments, you must also acknowledge the opposition and refute its main points. Some writers do this at the beginning of the article; others do it in the middle or near the end of the body of the article. Mentioning opposing arguments makes your work stronger by showing that you are aware of all sides of the discussion and can still make a strong case for your point of view.

The particular challenge of op-ed writing is that the writer must make the case in a very limited space, often no more than 500 words. Thus, an op-ed article requires a special kind of disciplined writing in which arguments and evidence must be marshalled very concisely to make your point. You must also refrain from mistreating your opposition. Attack the arguments, but stay away from making personal attacks on your opponent's character or reputation.

Conclusion

At the end of an op-ed article, restate your main point to leave a lasting impression on the reader. If you want the readers to react in a particular way, make your suggestions very strongly. For example, an op-ed article may encourage readers to vote a particular way on an issue, write their Member of Parliament, or boycott a particular product.

GETTING INTO PRINT

Writing an op-ed article will have little impact if it does not appear in print. If you want your article to be published, check the website of the newspaper or contact its editorial department to find out what the particular guidelines are. Be sure to follow these guidelines closely. For example, if the guidelines specify a particular length, do not exceed it, hoping that you will be granted an exception. Read a number of op-ed articles in target newspapers to get a sense of what a newspaper may be looking for. Develop a sense of how more-seasoned writers have been successful in making clear arguments in a very concise format.

RESOURCES

How to Write Op-Eds and Other Non-Fiction Articles

http://www.internet-resources.com/writers/wrlinks-nonfiction. htm#op-ed

 Keys to an op-ed assignment

- Maintain a clear, strong point of view
- Make good use of the argumentative style
- Make an emotional connection to the audience
- Use reader-friendly language—not language that is too specialized or academic
- Check your facts (your support must be accurate)
- Mention the opposing arguments and defuse them
- Finish with a strong conclusion

 Avoid

- Criticizing without adequate support
- Using logical fallacies and faulty argumentation
- Using language that is too specialized
- Selling a product rather than changing a viewpoint (for example: "Obesity could be eliminated if we all took EZE vitamins.")
- Making pejorative, insulting, or libellous statements about the opposition

LITERATURE REVIEW AND ANNOTATED BIBLIOGRAPHY

CONDUCTING A LITERATURE REVIEW

Any time you engage in research, you will have to do a study of the relevant literature on the topic. For some assignments, this review will simply provide the background to your research. In more advanced courses, a formal literature review may constitute an independent piece of research in itself.

A literature review is different from a literature survey. A survey simply records as accurately as possible what material is available. In contrast, a review is both a critical analysis of the themes found within the literature and an assessment of the state of the field of research on the particular topic. A literature review gives a comprehensive account of what has been published by academics and researchers on a specific topic.

Why do researchers conduct a literature review? A thorough literature review is a key component to any successful thesis or dissertation. In many cases, the literature review will serve as the introduction to a research paper, policy analysis paper, thesis, or dissertation. In the case of such longer pieces of research as theses or dissertations, the literature review explains why you chose your particular research topic and why you are adopting a particular approach. It also clarifies the concepts and definitions you are using as the basis for the study.

The first step in a literature review is narrowing the research topic and having a guiding question or focus in mind. For example, a literature review of Canadian foreign policy would be a massive undertaking and would leave the researcher wading through enormous amounts of material with no idea what to focus on. Even to narrow the topic to Canadian immigration policy would still leave a daunting task. Start by brainstorming, organizing the material, and selecting a more defined focus, such as Canadian refugee policy since World War II.

As a second step, you need to look for answers to a number of general questions about your topic. You can answer these questions by conducting a thorough literature review. Some of your questions should include the following:

- What is the current state of knowledge on this issue?
- What are the principal sources of information and data?
- What are the basic concepts and theories that are used in understanding this issue?
- Who are the recognized authorities on this subject?
- What methods have been used to study this topic?
- What controversies surround the study and understanding of this topic?
- What issues and questions remain to be studied and explored?

Use these general questions as a guide to formulate specific questions about your topic. For example, an application of these general questions to the topic of Canadian refugee policy since World War II might look something like this:

- How has refugee policy been defined?
- How has Canadian refugee policy evolved over time?

- What factors have researchers identified in explaining refugee policy?
- Do these explanations appear satisfactory, or is there a need to explore some alternative explanations?
- Are there developments in refugee policy that researchers have not yet studied? For example, there are studies that focus on the treatment of certain groups, such as Jews or communist dissidents, in Canadian immigration policy, but what about other minority groups?

Your third step is to survey information. Look for literature that gives an overview or summary of the topic. Some journals, like the *International Studies Review*, regularly publish articles that give a quick overview of the field and may assist you in narrowing your focus. As soon as possible, begin narrowing your focus to something manageable.

At this point, you are not reading the articles in close detail but just skimming them to get a sense of their approach to the topic or their principal findings. As you read, you will begin to see certain patterns emerge that will help you further define your topic. You will begin to get a sense of the principal issues involved, the prominent themes, the defining studies in the field, and the questions that are open to debate.

Keeping careful track of bibliographic information is essential at this point. Organizing source material into subject headings can save time later. For example, headings for a study on Canadian refugee policy since World War II might include historical background, primary government documents, statistical analysis, major events triggering policy change, refugee groups, and public or government opposition to changes.

The fourth step is a critical analysis of your findings. Go back to the questions you generated at the beginning of your research and start formulating general answers. Take careful notes on the sources you have chosen. Again, the aim is not to summarize in detail the findings but to tease out the dominant themes, contentious issues, and unanswered questions. Be sure to note which sources treat various aspects of the research question and which ones cover a broader spectrum of the field. You will now form a critical opinion of the worth of each resource. You can base your opinion both on what others have said and on your own analysis of the research materials.

The final step in a literature review is to write up your findings in an essay style. To do this, you need to decide whether your literature review is one part of a larger work, like a chapter on the background of a problem, or a document presented on its own as a research project. In the case of a thesis or dissertation, a literature review is an essential element that is used to show why your research is different from other works already published.

Keys to a literature review

- Define the topic
- Generate questions
- Consult a wide variety of source materials
- Create a survey of what literature is available
- Organize your findings into logical divisions
- Do a critical analysis of your findings to determine what has already been explored
- Write up your findings to fit the document

 Avoid

- Writing a paper about the topic instead of reviewing the literature
- Looking at only a few sources
- Researching too broad or too narrow a topic

For examples of literature reviews, see Columbia International Affairs On-line (CIAO), a database that contains hundreds of literature review documents in all fields of political science. This database is available through your university library.

For more information on how to do a literature review, see the following websites:

http://library.ucsc.edu/ref/howto/literaturereview.html

http://www.deakin.edu.au/library/findout/research/litrev.php

COMPILING AN ANNOTATED BIBLIOGRAPHY

Normally, a literature review will have a comprehensive bibliography of the research reviewed. In some cases, the researcher may want to take this a step further by preparing an annotated bibliography.

An annotated bibliography is more than just a list of resources used for a research project; annotated bibliographies are about a particular subject and have a specific form to follow. Each entry requires an annotation that evaluates the significance of each resource and its relationship to the entire field. The annotations demonstrate that the researcher is knowledgeable in the field and enable the reader to follow the researcher's critical analysis. The annotations should be between 75 and 150 words. Annotation entries that are too short do not give a thorough analysis, while those that are too long lose the reader.

In making your list of annotated entries, make sure to check which style is appropriate for the topic, and follow the bibliographic forms carefully.

Annotated bibliographies that contain more than 25 entries are often divided into subdivisions. Some writers prefer a subdivision by format (books, journals, newspapers, government documents). However, you could also make logical divisions by topic.

An annotated bibliography may require a short introduction that explains the purpose and focus of the collection of entries. Whether or not you include an introduction, it is a good idea to formulate a statement of purpose; this keeps your research focused on the topic.

✓ Keys to an annotated bibliography

- Ensure that your documentation is accurate
- Set up the pages consistently
- Organize the material into divisions
- Write a precise description of the content and value of each entry

✗ Avoid

- Being repetitious or providing vague explanations (this book is about ...)
- Plagiarizing descriptions or contents
- Formatting sections inconsistently
- Including entries that are off-topic or irrelevant to the stated focus

For more information on how to do an annotated bibliography, see the following websites:

http://www.library.mun.ca/guides/howto/annotated_bibl.php

http://www.library.cornell.edu/olinuris/ref/research/skill28.htm

These sites can provide you with some examples of annotated bibliographies:

http://www.cceia.org/media/1065_EmpireBibilography-May2004.pdf

http://www.remember.org/educate/anbib1.html

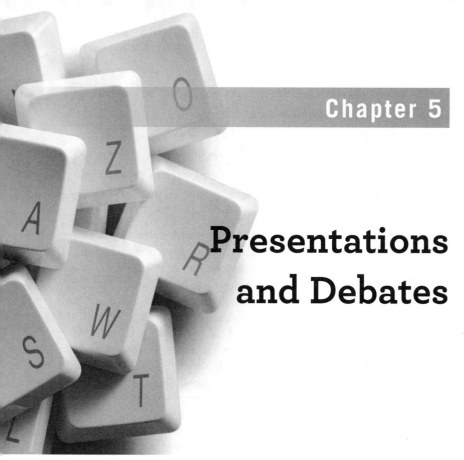

Chapter 5

Presentations
and Debates

Most political science courses require an oral assignment, either as a presentation or a debate. Both presentations and debates require research, organization, and practice. You will need to demonstrate both your knowledge of a topic and your communication skills in a public setting.

PRESENTATIONS

Presentations can take a variety of forms. Some presentations are individual; others are group assignments. Topics can vary from sharing information to arguing an ethical point. Most classroom presentations are shorter than 20 minutes. This means you have to focus clearly on the purpose of your presentation and three to four main points you want to get across. Ask yourself what major idea you want to communicate to the audience. Start by brainstorming the following items:

- Is this presentation informational or argumentative?
- Is this presentation part of a larger assignment such as a research paper?

- Who is the audience? How many people will be present?
- Is the audience familiar with this topic?
- How long is your presentation likely to be?
- Are you expected to use visuals like slides?
- What is the most important point you want to promote?
- Are you expected to answer questions from the audience during or after the presentation?

Answering the above questions will help you determine what research to do and how to organize the presentation. Informational presentations might explain a process or give a report on an organization or policy. Even though informational presentations are factual, they still need a key idea that the audience will remember. If the audience is not familiar with your topic, be prepared to explain key definitions and terms as well as giving additional background information. Argumentative presentations require a thesis statement or point that you are arguing. See the table below for examples of presentation types and example of topics for each. You must prepare a thesis statement and refute any possible counterarguments. (See Chapter 4 on argumentative writing.)

Your instructor may have designated minimum and maximum times for the presentation. Edit your ideas to fit into the time allotted while showing that you have done sufficient research on the topic.

RESEARCH

Researching for a presentation is much like researching information for a paper. Follow the guidelines for good research in Chapter 1. Always keep accurate records of your source material so you can create citations as necessary. Anticipate what questions your audience might have and be prepared to answer questions on any aspect of your topic. Use your research to decide a key idea for the presentation. This is much like writing a thesis statement for an essay. Even presentations that are informational need a strong main idea that unites the presentation. Here are some examples:

Topic	Type of Presentation	Thesis/Key Idea
How private members' bills are put forward in Parliament.	Informational/process	MPs who wish to introduce a private members' bill must follow a detailed process.

Topic	Type of Presentation	Thesis/Key Idea
Homelessness in Vancouver	Argumentative/ problem and solution	The B.C. government should take more responsibility for caring for the homeless in Vancouver by creating more low-cost housing in the downtown area.
Canadian aid to sub-Saharan Africa	Informational/report using statistics from various sources	Canadian aid to sub-Saharan Africa has decreased over the last five years.
Canadian aid to sub-Saharan Africa	Argumentative/ ethical	The decrease in aid to sub-Saharan Africa is a result of a deliberate shift in aid policy by the Conservative government. This shift unfairly promotes aid to more developed areas such as South America and endangers vital development projects.

Now follow through with your research. For both informational and argumentative presentations, you will need strong evidence such as statistics, policy documents, interviews, or reliable reports to back up your main idea.

ORGANIZATION

Organizing your research into a manageable presentation requires considering what type of pattern you will follow and shaping the content to your presentation format. Organizational patterns include chronological, descriptive, process, causal, problem/solution, classification, division, compare/contrast, analysis/criticism, and ethical. (See Chapter 3 for more detailed information.) Decide on which terms need a definition in order for the audience to understand the material. Create an outline and divide the material into major and minor points. Now you have a starting point to create a presentation.

One of the oldest pieces of advice for presentations is, "Tell them what you are going to tell them. Then tell them. Then tell them what you just told them." This is still an effective plan. Include an introduction with your main idea/argument and an idea of the order of discussion. The first two or three sentences will leave a lasting impression, good or bad, on the audience, so be prepared for a strong start. The body includes information that supports your key idea or thesis. Break your discussion into even divisions. Support each point with more than one source of evidence. If you are making a major argument on a point, insufficient evidence will not convince your audience. Conclude with a reminder of your main points and a strong statement of your argument. Compare these introductions and conclusions. Which examples do you feel are the most effective? Why?

Student A's presentation	Student B's presentation
I'm no expert, but I just want to give you guys an idea about how Twitter is affecting the outcome of elections.	Today we want to examine how using Twitter has affected the outcome of elections. First we will look at how Twitter can be used in elections, and then we will look at several specific examples.
So, uh, that's about all I have to say about Twitter and elections.	In conclusion, Twitter has made a significant difference in the outcome of elections on several levels. Twitter could be the most effective campaign tool of the future.

Keep a professional tone and make strong, direct statements throughout your presentation.

Using Visuals

Most visual presentations require a slide show as the most professional way to get information to the audience. Putting together a slide presentation takes time and some technical knowledge. First, check which specific programs are available, for example Microsoft PowerPoint or Apple Keynote. If you have never used presentation programs, check with your institution's student services or look for online tutorials. As you create your visuals, follow these general guidelines for a clear presentation:

1. Limit the number of slides and the amount of information on each slide. For each point on the screen, you will need to elaborate— add additional information during your presentation—rather than showing your entire text on the slide. Give the audience the main points and make them listen for the details. The "Golden Rule" of presentations is 6 × 7—that is six lines of text and no more than seven words per line on each slide. This rule is somewhat flexible, but remember to keep slides short and to the point.

Avoid slides that:

- Show too many words per line on each slide, and so are confusing

- Do not show points and sub points clearly

- Have a font size too small to read

- *If you use a script font, the audience might not be able to read it*

- USING ALL CAPITAL LETTERS IS NOT A GOOD IDEA

Keys for Creating Clear Slides:

- Show no more than six lines

- Use fewer than seven words per line

- Include one main idea per slide

- Use parallel bulleted points

- Use clear, readable fonts

- Show major and minor points clearly

2. Use parallel points whenever possible. Bulleted points are easier to understand when they are parallel. Here's an example:

Non-parallel

The causes for an increase in military spending are:

- Purchasing more helicopters

- Cost overruns on ships

- Travel and transportation costs have gone up

- They want to improve benefits for soldiers and their

  families

Parallel

The causes for an increase in military spending are:

- New purchases of helicopters

- Additional cost overruns for ships

- Increased costs for transportation

- Improved benefits for soldiers and their families

3. Be consistent with heading size. Use capital letters where necessary, but do not use all capital letters because it makes the print difficult to read. Make clear differences between headings (larger and bolder) and subheadings (same size and bold or italics).

4. Use contrasting colours and clear images. Using two colours of similar value (green and yellow) will result in unclear text. If you are using a variety of colours, test the contrast for clarity and readability.

5. Consider the size of the room when designing. The larger the room, the larger words and images must be on the screen in order for everyone to have a clear view. Always check the look of your presentation ahead of time. If you can't actually practice with a projector, stand at least two metres back from your computer monitor to check visibility and contrast.

6. Keep animations simple and consistent. Having your main points appear one at a time is useful, but it also means you have to use the controls more frequently during the presentation. Resist the temptation to use different types or complicated "fly-ins" during the presentation. Be consistent with how much information is presented at one time and do not make animation know-how the show point of the presentation.

7. Check links for video clips. You may wish to show a video clip from the Internet during your presentation. The links must work smoothly and quickly. Your audience does not want to wait while a YouTube clip gets started. Also make sure you check copyright permissions for any videos shown.

8. Keep charts and graphs simple. Do not put too much detailed information into one chart. Choose the type of visual that best shows your information (pie chart, line graph, bar graph). Create sharp charts and graphs with clear colours that showcase the most important information. Always show your sources at the bottom of the slide.

Use these websites for basic tutorials on PowerPoint presentations: http://www.dummies.com has excellent suggestions for all aspects of creating PowerPoint presentations.

http://gethelp.library.upenn.edu/workshops/biomed/ppt/open.html helps students create a variety of PowerPoint presentations.

Citations

Using images, showing charts or graphs, using video clips, or taking information from other sources requires that you use citations to acknowledge the origins of your information. Remember, the goal is to acknowledge your sources so your audience knows where the material came from. Use one of the following methods to credit your sources.

First, if you are distributing a handout, include a list of references used in APA, MLA, or other required style. If your presentation is being saved on a public site such as a course website, always include your references at the end.

Second, for visual presentations, include attributions directly on each slide. This is essential for images, charts, or graphs that you have taken from other sources. Acknowledgements can be shown in smaller print under each image, or in parentheses after a quotation.

Third, incorporate information into your presentation so your audience knows you are using cited information. Use starters like "according to Statistics Canada" or "In his new book, Tom Flanagan argues that" to indicate your sources. Create a list of references on your final slide.

For examples on how to include citations, see these websites:

http://plagiarism.umf.maine.edu/

http://www.ehow.com/how_7693024_cite-footnotes-powerpoint.html

http://www.ehow.com/how_5001942_use-apa-format-powerpoint.html

A final word about your handouts and on-screen work: do not forget to proofread!! Eliminate errors before they show up in front of an audience.

✓ Keys for good visual presentations

- Clear fonts and colours
- Limited amount on each screen
- Consistent headings and subheadings
- Minimum of special effects
- Large images
- Charts and graphs limited to essential "one idea" information
- Credit for information given
- Manageable technology
- Text free of grammar and spelling errors

✗ Avoid

- Busy fonts
- Too much information on one screen
- Unclear titles and subtitles
- Charts/graphs that are overloaded or too busy
- Small text or unclear images
- Plagiarism

PRACTICE

Presenting in front of a group takes practice. Poor presentations skills can sink even well-researched presentations. As your presentation takes shape, start rehearsing various sections to check on timing and ease of delivery. If you have created a long, complicated sentence with a number of multi-syllabic words, try revising into shorter sentences and easier words for better delivery. Determine the best way to handle your notes. Remember, you are not going to just read the text from your notes or the screen. It's your job to present an outline and elaborate on the information from your notes. Choose 3" × 5" note cards or other inconspicuous notes. If you are using a visual presentation, see if the program allows you to see both notes and screen material on a monitor. Practice your presentation including voice projection, eye contact, use of notes, gestures, pauses for effect, and movements. Don't forget to include transition words like first, second, next, and in conclusion as you move through your presentation. Keep your audience with you to the very end.

Getting the attention of your audience is challenging. Some common attention getters are asking an interesting question, presenting an unusual fact, or telling a personal anecdote. Move quickly from your opening into your main point for the presentation. Many speakers begin a presentation with a joke. Although these anecdotes and jokes create interest, be very careful in your choice of material. Inappropriate humour or anecdotes that do not relate to the topic must be avoided. Make sure your entire text is relevant to the topic. Don't get sidetracked as you are speaking.

Common errors in presenting

- Speaking too fast
- Pausing with "uh"
- Sounding nervous or breathless
- Looking only at notes or screen
- Fumbling, losing place in text
- Jumping from one idea to another without organization
- Apologizing, "I'm not very good at this"
- Letting technology get in the way: too many distractions, or unable to hook up
- Speaking too quietly, not projecting your voice to the entire audience
- Going over/under the allotted time
- Not getting the attention of the audience at the beginning
- Trailing off at the end without a clear conclusion
- Failing to include citations/credit for material used

Working with a Group

Some presentations are a group effort. Working together takes extra time and practice for a smooth, effective presentation. Once you have decided on who is in the group, take time to outline all the steps involved in the presentation. Determine who does what best and equalize the responsibilities. Set up a timeline for meetings and completed work. Rehearse the presentation several times. Your group must demonstrate that each member has done an equal part of the work.

Don't forget to practice introductions for each group member and handovers. The first part of your presentation should include introductions of each group member, the speaking order, and what material each speaker will cover. End each section with a "handover" phrase, and the next speaker begins with a "connector" that refers to the previous section. Some examples:

> **Handover:** *And now I'll turn it over to Ranjit, who will explain the effects of the lack of funding on infrastructure projects.*
>
> **Connector:** *As Tony has already mentioned, infrastructure projects in cities have not received funding as promised. This has had four major effects on Toronto.*
>
> **Handover:** *For the final section of our presentation, Amanda will share the conclusions of the taskforce on child poverty.*
>
> **Connector:** *As Sheila and Huang explained, the taskforce spent six months studying child poverty. Here are the major conclusions of that study.*

Successful presentations have an impact on the audience. If you have done your research, organized your material, and prepared carefully for each step, your presentation will be a success.

DEBATING THE ISSUES

One way to gain a more complete understanding of contemporary political issues is to participate in a classroom debate. Most students learn debating skills in a secondary school; some may have even joined debating teams or participated in a model United Nations forum. Political issues often take a yes/no format on a particular question. Debating at the college or university level requires a high level of preparation for both content and style. If you are asked to participate in a debate on political issues, the following guidelines will help you prepare for your part of the debate.

UNDERSTAND THE FORMAT OF THE DEBATE

Debates both in and beyond the classroom setting have several basic rules. One group presents the proposition or question. The other group presents a counterargument. Both sides have equal time to persuade the audience that their viewpoint is right. However, the format, time, and makeup of the team can vary according to which framework the debate is following. Are you debating as an individual or as a team? How much time is being allotted for each segment of the debate? Are you familiar with the rules of this debate? For example, is it acceptable to interrupt the other speakers?

Part of your preparation depends on the audience. Is this debate in the classroom or in front of a larger group? Your audience should be somewhat familiar with the topic, but you still need to present strong evidence to back up your point of view. You might be asked to defend an unpopular viewpoint, so you will need strong persuasive techniques as a part of your presentation. If possible, listen to some actual debates and take notes on how arguments and counterarguments are presented.

What do you hope to achieve from this debate? Classroom debates are most often evaluated on the quality of analysis, strength of the evidence, organization, and delivery skills. A key component of any debate is to analyze your strengths and weaknesses in each of these areas.

For more information on the various debate formats, see the websites listed at the end of this chapter.

UNDERSTAND THE QUESTION

Most debates put forward a question or proposition that has a yes/no or agree/disagree idea. Debaters should start by researching both sides of the question. Start with sources listed in course texts and then research other reliable sources as a part of your preparation. Debating relies on critical thinking. Evaluate sources, analyze the arguments, and synthesize materials. You may be asked to defend a position that you do not personally agree with. In any debate, keep an open mind to all arguments.

FORMULATE ARGUMENTS AND COUNTERARGUMENTS

Whatever side you are asked to support, your knowledge of both sides of the question is crucial to success. Make a list of the important points on each side of the argument. You must be ready to support your claims as well as anticipate all opposing arguments and refute them. What are the important types of evidence for each claim? Citing more than one piece of evidence to back up your points strengthens your arguments. Evaluate all evidence for strengths and weaknesses. Use only reliable sources such as peer-reviewed journals, expert researchers, and trustworthy websites. Relying on Wikipedia for information or analysis is not professional. Keep careful records of all your research sources. You may need these for future debates or follow up assignments on the topic.

Develop clear lines of reasoning. Identify any logical fallacies in your own thinking and be ready to attack your opponents if you observe any fallacies in their presentation. For more information on logical fallacies, see "Writing-Style FAQs" in Chapter 3.

Most importantly, teams must organize each segment of their presentations to avoid repetition. Decide ahead of time what the strongest arguments and evidence are. Ideally, your team should reiterate the strongest points in the closing arguments. Always conclude with a strong summary of your position.

PREPARE AND PRACTICE

Because most debates consist of teamwork, preparation and rehearsal are important. Practice keeping within time limits and changing from one speaker to another. Teams should agree in advance on how to handle unexpected arguments from the other side.

Refresh your memory on all the qualities of good public speaking:

- Good eye contact
- Appropriate mannerisms
- Natural gestures
- Vocal variety
- Voice projection appropriate for the setting
- Speaking from cues
- Appropriate business dress if required

During practice sessions, use peer review to identify negative points of your debating skills such as:

- Boring delivery or monotone voice
- Hesitation or usage of "um" or "uh"
- Lack of eye contact
- Speaking too loudly, too quietly, or too quickly
- Obvious nervousness

In addition, check out the room and the sound equipment if necessary. Make sure your team is comfortable with the seating arrangements and the electronics.

DURING THE DEBATE

Rehearsing will help your team move smoothly through the debate. The most important task is to listen and jot down notes during the other teams' presentation. You will have to think of quick rejoinders for their arguments. Be ready to challenge their reasoning and evidence on a point-by-point basis. Stay focused and follow the rules. Don't personalize the arguments. Launching a personal attack on the opposing team will sink your credibility immediately.

AFTER THE DEBATE

Whatever the outcome, your team should take time to debrief. Analyze the content and style. Jot down points of interest from both sides of the question. What has your team gained from this experience? What could you do better the next time? Remember, the objective of most debating exercises is to gain knowledge about a particular issue.

 Keys to debating

- Know the format
- Understand the question
- Research the topic thoroughly
- Formulate a strong position
- Use team work to prepare
- Practice good speaking skills
- Anticipate rebuttals

 Avoid

- Attacking the person rather than the issue
- Speaking off the topic
- Pausing or saying "um"
- Appearing unprepared
- Looking unprofessional

For more information, see:

Basic Debating Skills

http://www.actdu.org.au/archives/actein_site/basicskills_.html

Holding Your Own Debate

http://www.actdu.org.au/archives/actein_site/owndebate_.html

Debating Formats and Actual Recorded Debates

http://debate.uvm.edu/

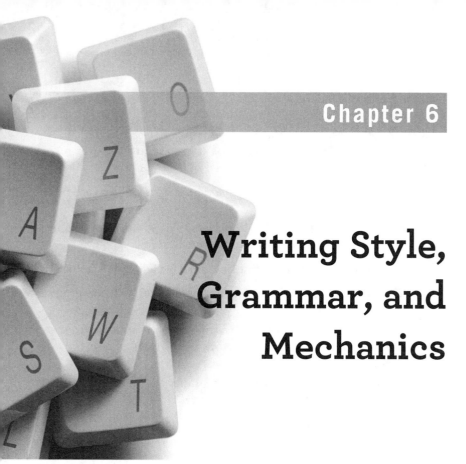

Chapter 6

Writing Style, Grammar, and Mechanics

Good research, careful analysis, and accurate documentation are all important parts of excellent writing in political science. However, poor writing style and incorrect grammar can detract from your work and lower your mark considerably. This chapter looks at three elements of good writing: writing style, grammar, and mechanics. Mastering these elements will add polish to your assignments. At the end of this chapter, you will find a list of online resources for additional assistance.

WRITING STYLE

Good writing style doesn't just happen when you create a paragraph or essay. Writers need to edit and revise sentences and paragraphs for clarity and variety. As you revise your work, identify and change sentences that are weak or need improvement in writing style. The following section gives you guidance on writing for clarity and variety.

CHOOSE VERBS CAREFULLY

Verb tenses tell the reader when something happens. Using correct and consistent verb tenses adds clarity to your work. Descriptions and facts need present tense. Use present tense for stating an argument or research findings from current authors and reports.

- *Lloyd Axworthy argues that human security is still relevant in developing countries.*
- *The recent report from the World Food Programme warns that food shortages in the Sudan are becoming severe.*

Use present tense to describe current situations including policies or laws.

- *Municipalities get extra funding for major transportation projects from the provinces.*
- *The prime minister recommends candidates for justices of the Supreme Court; the governor general usually approves without question.*
- *Florida's "Stand Your Ground" law states that individuals may defend themselves with force if attacked.*

Use past tenses when discussing events or ideas that occurred in the past, including historical events, past laws or practices, and writings of non-contemporary authors.

- *Canada's immigration laws during World War II excluded many Jewish refugees from Eastern Europe.*
- *Sir John A. Macdonald believed that a national railway was important to Canada's economy.*

Use present perfect tense to show ongoing events or a continuation of an action.

- *Canada has supported the Responsibility to Protect policy, but has not always had sufficient influence at the United Nations to enforce it.*
- *Environmental concerns over further development of the oil sands have created divisions among the MLAs.*

Use modal verbs to show possibility and speculation.

- *The deadline for troop withdrawal might be extended beyond 2014.*
- *Although the polls indicate a majority government, the outcome on election day may be quite different.*

Know the difference between active voice and passive voice. Sentences in active voice are stronger and more direct than those in the passive voice. Compare these sentences:

Passive: *The accounts were reviewed by the Auditor General and recommendations were made to improve accountability.*

Active: *The Auditor General reviewed the accounts and made recommendations to improve accountability.*

Passive voice may be appropriate in some writing, but make sure you have a good reason for using it. For more information on using active and passive voice see the grammar resources at the end of the chapter.

MAKE YOUR SENTENCES PARALLEL

Revise sentences for parallel structure. Sentence elements such as nouns, verbs, and phrases should use the same grammatical pattern.

Error: *The MLAs got feedback from their constituents and the legislation was discussed before they passed the bill.*

Corrected: *The MLAs got feedback from their constituents, discussed changes to the legislation, and finally passed the bill before adjourning.*

If you use bulleted points in your discussion, create a list with parallel points:

Political science students should be able to

- *distinguish opinion from fact*
- *recognize logical fallacies in arguments*
- *use both inductive and deductive reasoning*
- *compare opposing arguments*

ELIMINATE WORDINESS AND REDUNDANCIES

Writing clear sentences includes checking for excessive wordiness and redundant meanings. Becoming familiar with a list of common wordiness problems will help you cut out unnecessary words in writing. One such list is found at the University of Victoria's writing centre website (http://web.uvic.ca/~gkblank/wordiness.html). The following sentences contain a few examples of wordiness:

Wordy: *The food aid shipments were delayed until such time as the military secured the roads.*

Revised: *The food aid shipments were delayed until the military secured the roads.*

Wordy: *Election officials did not announce a winner due to the fact that fewer than 10 votes separated the two candidates. The recount will happen in the not too distant future.*

Revised: *Election officials did not announce a winner because fewer than 10 votes separated the two candidates. The recount will happen soon.*

Redundancies are expressions that say the same thing twice.

- *The dissatisfied workers gave no warning in advance of their illegal strike.* (Remove *in advance*)
- *A couple of the new MPs are young in age.* (Remove *in age*)

Evaluate all sentences beginning with there is/are, there was/were, or it is/was. Revise to create a clear sentence.

Wordy: *It is clear that the prime minister's office must take responsibility for these scandalous leaks.*

Revised: *The prime minister's office must take responsibility for these scandalous leaks.*

Wordy: *There were three MPs who were elected by fewer than 100 votes.*

Revised: *Three MPS were elected by fewer than 100 votes.*

Revise sentences containing *is when… is where…* and *the reason is because…* Do not use *is when* or *is where* for definitions.

Error: *Filibuster is when MPs attempt to block legislation by carrying on an endless debate.*

Revised: *Filibuster is a long debate by MPs attempting to block legislation.*

Error: *The Responsibility to Protect is where one country intervenes to protect citizens in another country.*

Revised: *The Responsibility to Protect is a policy of the United Nations designed to permit one country to intervene to protect citizens of another country.*

USE A VARIETY OF SENTENCE STYLES

Good writers avoid using all short or all long sentences. Use a variety of sentence styles to keep your work interesting. These sentences are examples of the different sentence styles.

Simple sentence: *Untreated mental illness is a major cause of homelessness.*

Compound sentence: *Untreated mental illness is a major cause of homelessness, so the municipalities welcomed provincial funding for drop-in care centres.*

Complex sentence: *Although untreated mental illness is a major cause of homelessness, other factors such as poverty and drug addiction are contributing factors.*

Avoid the temptation to make all sentences long just to sound more formal. Sentences with too many dependent clauses may obscure the main idea. Any sentence longer than three lines of type should be revised.

Error: *Although untreated mental illness is a major cause of homelessness, other factors such as poverty and drug addiction are contributing factors which are being studied by the researchers who received funding from the provincial government's health initiatives program.*

Revised: *Although untreated mental illness is a major cause of homelessness, other factors such as poverty and drug addiction are contributing factors. Funding from the provincial government's health initiatives program has enabled researchers to study these factors.*

USE TRANSITION WORDS

Using clear transition words keeps your writing on track as you progress from one idea to another. Use transition words at the beginning of and within paragraphs. Here are some of the most common transitions:

Sequence: *first, second, third, next, finally*

Time: *after, as, next, later, meanwhile, then, when, while, immediately*

Addition: *also, besides, further, furthermore, in addition, next, too*

Contrast: *but, however, in contrast, nevertheless, although, yet*

Reason: *therefore, consequently, thus, as a result, because, since*

For a complete list of commonly used transitions in writing, see http://jc-schools.net/write/transition.htm

GRAMMAR

Good writing includes editing for good grammar. The following section gives brief examples of the most common grammar errors in writing. Your grammar checker may indicate you have one or more of the following problems. Refer to grammar assistance websites for complete information on how to correct these common grammar errors.

SENTENCE STRUCTURE

Sentence structure errors include run-ons, fragments, comma splices, and modifier problems. Run-on or fused sentences are two independent thoughts that run together without any punctuation or coordination. Correct run-ons by using a period, semicolon, coordinating conjunction, or subordinating clause.

> **Error:** *The major focus of the aid program was to provide clean drinking water to villages in the Congo only 25 percent of inhabitants have safe water.*

> **Corrected:** *The major focus of the aid program was to provide clean drinking water to villages in the Congo where only 25 percent of inhabitants have safe water.*

Sentence fragments are an incomplete idea. Some fragments need to be joined to another sentence; other fragments need a clear subject and complete verb. Remember, even though a sentence looks long, it may be a fragment.

> **Error:** *Although Greenpeace has thoroughly researched the decline in the whale population on the West Coast and submitted a written report.*

> **Corrected:** *Although Greenpeace has thoroughly researched the decline in the whale population on the West Coast and submitted a written report, the group has failed to consider Aboriginal hunting rights.*

Fragments starting with "which" are particular problems to watch out for.

> **Error:** *Statistics Canada recently reported on the number of Aboriginal communities without safe drinking water. Which surprised the Minister of Northern Affairs.*

> **Corrected:** *Statistics Canada recently reported on the number of Aboriginal communities without safe drinking water; these facts surprised the Minister of Northern Affairs.*

Comma splices occur when two independent clauses are joined by a comma instead of a semicolon or coordinating conjunction.

> **Error:** *Germany argued for more stringent economic reforms, France disagreed.*

> **Corrected with a semicolon:** *Germany argued for more stringent economic reforms; France disagreed.*

Corrected with a coordinating conjunction: *Germany argued for more stringent economic reforms, but France disagreed.*

Modifiers are sometimes misplaced in the sentence, causing confusion in the meaning of the sentence. Correct these errors by placing the modifier close to the phrase or clause it modifies. In the following example, keeping the subject (Congo) close to the verb (reverted) makes the sentence much clearer.

Error: *The Democratic Republic of the Congo, after a name change to Zaire that lasted 26 years, reverted to its former name in 1997.*

Corrected: *After a name change to Zaire that lasted 26 years, the Democratic Republic of the Congo reverted to its former name in 1997.*

Error: *Quinn (2010), in her article on restorative justice, argues for hearings for both victims and perpetrators.*

Revised: *In her article on restorative justice, Quinn (2010) argues for hearings for both victims and perpetrators.*

Dangling modifiers may introduce an action without saying who or what the subject is. This type of error leads to confusion; readers do not know who is doing the action. Correct these errors by revising the sentence to clarify the actor. The following example needs revision because the ornate carvings are not doing the action.

Error: *When entering the Library of Parliament, the ornate carvings are striking.*

Corrected: *When I entered the Library of Parliament, I was struck by the ornate carvings.*

Error: *Winning the Republican nomination for president, admirers waited to greet Mitt Romney.*

Corrected: *Admirers waited to greet Mitt Romney who had just won the Republican nomination for president.*

SUBJECT/VERB AGREEMENT

Most writers can recognize simple problems with subject/verb agreement in the present tense. However, several fairly common problems can occur, including words that come between the subject and the verb, subjects joined with or/nor, and indefinite pronouns as a subject.

In the following example, the word *results* is the subject, so the verb must be plural.

Error: *The results of the UNESCO report is being challenged.*

Corrected: *The results of the UNESCO report are being challenged.*

Check subjects joined by *either/or* and *neither/nor* combinations. The subject closest to the verb determines the agreement. If one subject is singular and the other is plural, writers usually put the plural subject second.

Error: *Neither the administrative assistants nor the manager have access to the coded information.*

Corrected: *Neither the manager nor the administrative assistants have access to the coded information.*

Indefinite pronouns are words such as anybody, each, either, everything, neither, or someone. These words do not refer to a specific person or thing; they take a singular verb in formal writing.

Error: *Each of the participants have been carefully screened.*

Corrected: *Each of the participants has been carefully screened.*

PRONOUN ERRORS

In formal writing, a pronoun must agree with its antecedent. Common pronoun errors in writing include agreement with indefinite pronouns and ambiguous or vague references.

Indefinite pronouns are singular and use singular pronouns. In the example below, *each candidate* is singular and *their* is plural.

Error: *Each candidate has their own campaign office.*

Corrected: *Each candidate has his or her own campaign office.*

To avoid overuse or awkwardness with his/her, change the subject of the sentence to plural.

Corrected: *All candidates have their own campaign offices.*

Ambiguous or vague references occur when a pronoun does not have a clear antecedent, or the pronoun is too far away from the noun in the writing. Correct these errors by adding or repeating the noun. In the following example, *them* does not clearly refer to any noun. Add the noun for clarity.

Error: *When updating the report, Sam revised them to include the latest statistics.*

Corrected: *When updating the report, Sam revised the figures to include the latest statistics.*

Check pronoun references using *this, that, which,* and *it.* These words must refer to a specific noun, not to an entire sentence.

Error: *The voter turn-out was more than 65 percent, and the NDP won the seat, which was surprising.*

Change the sentence to show which idea is surprising.

Corrected: *Surprisingly, the voter turn-out was more than 65 percent, and the NDP won the seat.*

Corrected: *The voter turn-out was more than 65 percent, and the NDP upset surprised political pundits.*

MECHANICS

In each draft of your paper, you will catch errors and typos, such as misspelled words and faulty punctuation. The spell checker and grammar checker in your word-processing program can help you identify many of these errors. However, they will not catch everything. You should carefully read your final draft to eliminate errors in mechanics. The following information is a general guide for the rules of capitalization and punctuation.

GENERAL GUIDELINES FOR CAPITALIZATION

Capitalize the first word in every sentence:

- *The losing candidate wanted to thank all her supporters.*

Capitalize the first word of a sentence in a direct quotation:

- *The auditor pressed for information by asking, "Did you keep a daily record of your receipts?"*

However, do not capitalize the first word of a quotation that is integrated into your sentence:

- *The auditor reprimanded the committee chair for claiming "entertainment expenditures well beyond the limit."*

If the first word of a sentence is a number, write out the number and capitalize it:

- *Twenty-seven new judges took the oath of office.*

For people, capitalize these words:

- names and nicknames: Navejoit, Navie, William, Bill
- words referring to ethnic origin and language: Canadian, French, Chinese

- titles associated with a name: Ms. Jefferson, Mr. Sandhu, Dr. Wong, Rev. McGregor, Prince William, Prime Minister Harper, Saint Peter, Uncle Richard, and Grandmother Bailey
- abbreviated credentials coming after a name: Jeremy Bighorse, M.D., Zainab Ayoub, Ph.D.

Capitalize **proper nouns**:

- the days of the week, months of the year, and holidays: Sunday, January 2, Christmas
- the planets and other named objects in space (but not the sun and the moon): Mercury, the Milky Way, Titan
- the names of organizations: the Red Cross, Microsoft, Lionsgate Productions
- political parties and government departments: the Conservative Party of Canada, Health Canada, Service Canada
- historical events: World War II, the Restoration
- geographic names, such as countries, rivers, mountains, cities, and bodies of water: the Mackenzie River, Mount Norquay, Lake Erie
- religions, both as nouns and as adjectives: Christianity, Christian, Judaism, Jewish, Buddhist, Muslim, Hindu, Taoism
- the names of specific courses at school: Political Science 101, Philosophy 230
- the informal greeting and closing of a letter: Dear Mavis, Sincerely

Capitalize **common abbreviations:**

- BCE and CE (or their equivalents, BC and AD); in some style guides, these appear in small capitals: BCE, CE, BC, AD
- countries, provinces and territories, and states: UK, PEI, NY
- organizations: UNICEF, NATO, CAA, CBC
- other accepted abbreviations: HIV/AIDS, DART, MLA

Special Notes for Essay Writers

Documenting sources in a works cited list or bibliography requires careful attention to capitalization. Check the citation guides in Chapter 3 for complete formats.

QUICK GUIDE TO PUNCTUATION

Correct punctuation is an essential element of quality student writing. While some computer programs will indicate punctuation problems, writers should edit carefully to avoid punctuation errors.

The following are basic guidelines for punctuation. For complete rules, check the list of style guides and online references listed at the end of this chapter.

Periods

Use periods at the end of statements and with abbreviations:

- *The third reading of the bill took place on April 16, 2012.*
- *Mr. Hernandez and Ms. Tran registered a number of complaints concerning the new zoning for Fairview Ave.*
- *The event ended promptly at 11 p.m.*

Note: Do not double a period at the end of the sentence. If an abbreviation occurs at the end, do not add an extra period.

Pay special attention to periods in parenthetical documentation. The period comes after the last parenthesis:

- *Although the committee investigated the complaints, they did not recommend any solutions to the problem (Sanders, 2010, p. 127).*

Question Marks

Question marks are used only for direct questions; therefore, they are seldom used in academic writing and reporting, except for rhetorical questions and quotations:

- *Are you ready to hear the results of the investigation?*
- *Why did the prime minister delay making a decision?*
- *The committee chair asked, "Why didn't the minister report his findings immediately?"*

Do not use a question mark with an indirect question:

- *The committee asked why the minister hadn't reported his findings immediately.*

Exclamation Points

An exclamation point indicates shock, surprise, or extreme excitement, so it is rarely used in formal writing:

- *More than 200 000 people were killed by the tsunami!*

Instead, good writers use vivid vocabulary to communicate strong feelings:

- *Tragically, more than 200 000 people were killed by the most devastating tsunami ever recorded.*

Commas

The comma is the most frequently used punctuation mark, so it is essential to practice good comma usage.

Separate the elements of dates and addresses with a comma:

- *September 16, 2011*
- *Saturday, February 26, 2012*
- *Fort Erie, Ontario, Canada*

Note that MLA style inverts the order of the elements in a date: 16 September 2011. In this case, commas are not used to separate the elements.

Set off a long introductory phrase with a comma:

- *In the prime minister's absence, the deputy prime minister answered the question.*
- *At the beginning of her career, Ms. Epstein was a political appointee.*

Use a comma when a dependent adverbial clause precedes a main clause:

- *When the supplies had been assembled, the unit left for Afghanistan.*
- *Instead of responding directly, the MLA referred the matter to her assistant.*

Use commas to set off transitional words and expressions:

- *Skim milk powder and dried eggs, for example, were added to food aid because of pressure from Canadian farmers.*

Use commas to set off nonessential information:

- *Jack Layton, the former leader of the NDP, left a legacy of political activism characterized by compassion for the common people.*

Note: Nonessential information is also called non-restrictive information. Check sources at the end of this chapter for complete information on nonessential items in a sentence.

Separate three or more items in a list with commas:

- *Martina's areas of expertise include tax law, international finance, and trade agreements.*

- *The lobbyist made strong efforts to decrease taxation on oil companies, reduce the amount of paperwork to complete applications, and shorten the length of time required for environmental assessments.*

Note: Some disagreement still exists on whether to use a comma before the final element in a list in informal writing. However, all major style guides require a comma before *and* in a series.

Use commas to separate independent clauses (complete sentences) that are joined by a coordinating conjunction. The conjunctions are *and, but, yet, so, or, nor, for*:

- *It's doubtful that he will win his appeal, but his lawyer will try.*

Separate some elements in bibliographic entries with a comma. However, citation styles vary, so consult the section on citation styles or various style guides for the correct forms.

Common mistakes in the use of commas

A comma cannot be used alone to separate two independent clauses:

Error: *It's doubtful that he will win his appeal, his lawyer will try.*

Repair this error by using a conjunction or a semicolon:

Corrected: *It's doubtful that he will win his appeal, but his lawyer will try.*

A comma is not needed before an adverbial clause at the end of the sentence:

- *She voted NDP for the first time because she was impressed by their childcare policies.*

(Do not put a comma after the word *time*.)

A comma should not separate a subject from its verb:

Error: *Most of the international studies students, indicated they had visited developing countries.*

Corrected: *Most of the international studies students indicated they had visited developing countries.*

A comma should not separate two equal words or phrases joined by *and*:

Error: *Many of the students had already fulfilled the requirements in English, and French.*

Corrected: *Many of the students had already fulfilled the requirements in English and French.*

Commas should not set off essential information (restrictive clauses). Restrictive and non-restrictive clauses can be confusing. Check a grammar manual for a thorough explanation.

Error: *All the countries, that supported the resolution, were ready to contribute ground troops for six months.*

Corrected: *All the countries that supported the resolution were ready to contribute ground troops for six months.*

A comma should not be used between verbs in a compound predicate (two or more verbs that have the same subject):

Error: *The governor general visits different parts of Canada, and hosts events at Rideau Hall.*

Corrected: *The governor general visits different parts of Canada and hosts events at Rideau Hall.*

Semicolons

Semicolons are most often used to separate independent clauses. However, the two clauses must demonstrate a relationship:

- *Her election campaign is failing badly; the team needs to develop new strategies.*

Semicolons can separate clauses joined by transitional words or expressions:

- *The research and development team proposed six new ideas; however, the company considered only two of them.*

Semicolons separate items in a list that already contain commas. The semicolons make the list easier to read:

- *Attendees from the First Nations included Susan Harris, Mi'kmaq Confederacy of PEI; Grand Chief Matthew Coon Come, Grand Council of the Cree; and Chief Charles Weaselhead, Tsuu T'ina nation.*

Colons

Colons call attention to what comes after the colon. In a sentence, a colon can signal the start of a quotation, a restatement, or a list only if a complete sentence precedes the colon.

Quotation

- *The investigating committee found proof of what a senior official had said: "The department had a deficit and we needed to find creative ways to finance the projects."*

Restatement

- *Decisions of the Supreme Court are final: no further appeals can be made.*

List

- *There are three prerequisites for the political studies program: English 101, Philosophy 200, and Geography 103.*

Special uses of the colon in essay writing and documentation

Use a colon between titles and subtitles, even if the colon doesn't appear in the original work:

- *Aid and Ebb Tide: A History of CIDA and Canadian Development Assistance.*

Use a colon between place of publication and the publishing company name in bibliographic entries:

- *Waterloo, Ontario: Wilfrid Laurier Press, 2007.*

Other uses of the colon

Use a colon between the hours and minutes when showing time:

- *The flight departs at 6:35 p.m.*

Use a colon in formal letters and memos:

- *Dear Madam:*
- *To: David Bailey*
- *Subject: Cost overruns*
- *cc: Jasmine Dayal*

Use a colon between chapters and verses of the Bible:

- *Psalm 23:2*

Apostrophes

Apostrophes show possession, indicate contractions, and form special kinds of plurals.

Use an apostrophe and an *s* to show possession of singular nouns and indefinite pronouns:

- *Taylor's report contained shocking statistics.*
- *This was not anyone's idea of efficient usage of time.*
- *Jillian Deschamps's application was accepted at UBC.*

For plural nouns, put the apostrophe after the *s*:

- *Hackers were able to break the code on several legislators' computers.*

For irregular plurals that do not end in *s*, add both an apostrophe and an *s*:

- *After seeing the children's plight, numerous donors gave generously to the Red Cross.*

Use an apostrophe only on the final noun to indicate joint possession:

- *Maynard and Sandra's farm was included in the land claim settlement.*

Make all nouns possessive to show individual possession:

- *Although they are identical twins, Eli's and Matthew's grades in math are very different.*

Use apostrophes to indicate letters that are left out when forming contractions:

- *doesn't, aren't, wouldn't, there's*

Note: Contractions are not normally used in formal writing.

Use apostrophes for some kinds of plurals, including letters:

- *Amanda got five A's and two B's on her report card.*

Note: Some styles use an apostrophe in such words as ABCs.

Use apostrophes in dates to replace the first two digits.

- *Interest rates were high in the '80s but declined substantially by the end of the '90s.*

Do not use an apostrophe at the end of the year to show plurals:

Error: *1990's*

Corrected: *1990s*

Most common mistake in the use of apostrophes

The most common error with the apostrophe is inserting one in the possessive from of *it*.

Error: *India has been able to grow all of it's own food for decades.*

Corrected: *India has been able to grow all of its own food for decades.*

It's is the contraction for *it is*. The word *its* indicates possession.

Another common error is using an apostrophe for the plurals of nouns:

Error: *Three director's were arrested for fraud.*

Corrected: *Three directors were arrested for fraud.*

Quotation Marks

Use double quotation marks with direct speech. Remember, direct speech uses the exact words of another person:

- *The Minister of Foreign Affairs said, "I have no knowledge of this particular case."*

Do not use quotation marks for indirect speech or paraphrases:

- *The Minister of Foreign Affairs said she had no knowledge of that particular case.*

Do not use quotation marks around block quotations. See "Incorporating Quotations, Paraphrases, and Summaries" in Chapter 3 for rules about inserting short and long quotations in the text.

Use double quotation marks to call attention to particular words in a sentence:

- *One feature of the 2012 presidential campaign was the use of "blogs" for information sharing.*

MLA citation style uses double quotation marks around the titles of shorter works: newspaper and journal articles, essays, speeches, chapters of a book, individual episodes of radio and television programs, songs, poems, and short stories:

- Smith, Graeme, and Estanislao Oziewicz. "CIDA's Rules May Hinder Food-Aid Efforts." *The Globe and Mail* 7 Jan. 2005: A3. Print.

Sometimes you need quotation marks within a quotation. Use a pair of single quotation marks to set off the new quote or title:

- *The aging veteran said, "Hearing the child recite 'In Flanders Fields' brought back so many memories of the war."*

Other punctuation with quotation marks

Commas and periods go *inside* quotation marks.

- *"It is true," he said, "that I was aware of the illegal payments."*

In MLA and APA citation style, parentheses enclosing citation information go outside quotation marks, followed by a period.

- *Charles Krauthammer argues that peacekeeping is an illusion in his article, "Peacekeeping Is for Chumps" (289).*

Semicolons and colons go outside the quotation marks.

- *Eighty percent of the students failed to identify the author of "I Have a Dream": Dr. Martin Luther King.*

Question marks and exclamation points go inside quotation marks when they are a part of the quoted material:

- *The debate for next week is "Do Biological Differences Predispose Men to War?"*

Question marks and exclamation points go outside the quotation marks if they apply to the entire sentence:

- *What do you think about the reading "Peacekeeping Is for Chumps"?*

Brackets and Parentheses

Put parentheses around information such as documented sources or nonessential information. Use them to enclose numbers or letters in a list that is run into the text:

- *The astounding number of deaths as a result of the tsunami (more than 200 000) will have an impact on the economies of the affected countries for years to come.*
- *The average day labourer earns only 600 rupees (CDN $12.00) per month.*
- *Aid workers to the devastated region should take a number of pre-cautions: (1) have a tetanus shot, (2) carry water purification tablets, (3) purchase a mosquito net, and (4) take anti-malarial drugs.*

Place square brackets around any material you add into a quotation for clarity. Use square brackets when a pronoun has no antecedent within the quotation. Adding the noun is essential:

- *"We felt elated when we saw him [Mubarak] on trial for his crimes. At last we knew that he would be punished."*

Ellipses

Ellipsis is the term for the omission of words from a quotation. The omission is indicated by three period dots with spaces between (...). It is not needed at the beginning or end of a quotation. Check the style manual you are following for the specific rules on placing an ellipsis in a quotation:

- *According to the report, "Although a wide variety of sanctions was imposed against South Africa ... these measures were never coordinated and their consistency of implementation was widely acknowledged to be uneven."*

Dashes

Use a dash to set off extra material in a sentence. Create a dash by typing two hyphens without any spaces before or after. Unlike commas and parentheses, dashes call the reader's attention to the extra material. Use dashes to highlight extra facts, explanations, or lists. Put dashes on both sides of material in the middle of the sentence. For insertions that end a sentence, use a dash at the beginning and end with a period:

- *Modern advances in technology—high-speed Internet and cell phone communication—have facilitated faster exchanges of information among intelligence agencies.*

- *Holocaust memorials serve two important functions—honouring the dead and reminding the living of our greatest human tragedy.*

Hyphens

Use hyphens in the following cases:

- in some compound words: *mother-in-law*
- in two or more words working as an adjective before a noun: *an eighty-year-old man, a hard-working citizen*
- in fractions and numbers: *one-fourth, twenty-six*
- in words that divide at the end of the line when this is not done automatically by a word-processing program (divisions occur only between syllables)
- between two identical vowels or consonants in some words: *anti-inflationary, co-opted*
- with the prefixes all-, ex-, great-, quasi-, and with the suffix -elect: *all-time, ex-premier, great-grandmother, quasi-official, president-elect*

Note: The prefix *self-* takes a hyphen in some words, as in *self-serving,* but not in other words, such as *selfless.* Spell checkers may correct these, but consult your dictionary for guidance.

Slashes

You can use a slash (or solidus) to separate two equal items, but use them sparingly (you could also use hyphens):

- *student/teacher conferences, accountant/manager*

Do not overuse slashes, especially for gender inclusiveness:

- *Every student wrote his/her own response.*

Rewrite with a plural pronoun: *All students wrote their own responses.*

Use slashes to separate elements in dates: *02/28/09*

A final note on punctuation: The spell checker and grammar checker functions of word-processing programs will correct some punctuation problems, but they are unlikely to catch all of them. Check writing guide books and websites for detailed information, or get assistance from a writing tutor.

ONLINE RESOURCES

The following online sources will help you with writing style, grammar, and mechanics. You also may wish to consult a writing tutor or the writing centre at your institution.

http://www.uottawa.ca/academic/arts/writcent/hypergrammar

http://grammar.ccc.commnet.edu/grammar/index2.htm

http://owl.english.purdue.edu

http://www.douglas.bc.ca/services/learning-centre/selfhelp/handouts.html

Appendix I

Sources to Consult

POLITICAL SCIENCE RESOURCES

POLITICAL SCIENCE JOURNALS

American Journal of Political Science

American Political Science Review

British Journal of International Studies

British Journal of Political Science

Canadian Journal of Political Science

Canadian Public Administration

Canadian Public Policy

Comparative Political Studies

Comparative Politics

Cooperation and Conflict

European Journal of Political Science

Foreign Affairs

Foreign Policy

Global Governance

Government and Opposition

History of Political Thought

Indian Journal of Political Science

International Affairs

International Organization

International Political Science Review

International Security

International Studies

International Studies Quarterly

Journal of Chinese Political Science

Journal of Conflict Resolution

Journal of Constitutional and Parliamentary Studies

Journal of European Integration

Journal of International Affairs

Journal of Modern African Studies

Journal of Peace Research

Journal of Political Economy

Journal of Politics

Journal of Public Policy

Journal of Women, Politics and Policy

Latin American Research Review

Legislative Studies Quarterly

Middle Eastern Studies

Millennium

Orbis: A Journal of World Affairs

Parliamentarian

Parliamentary Affairs

Peace Research

Perspectives on Political Science

Philosophy and Public Affairs

Policy Review

Policy Studies Journal

Policy Studies Review

Political Behaviour

Political Quarterly

Political Science

Political Science Quarterly

Political Science Review

Political Science Reviewer

Political Studies

Political Theory

Politics

Politics and Gender

Politics & Society

Public Administration Review

Public Choice

Public Interest

Public Opinion Quarterly

Publius: The Journal of Federalism

Review of International Studies

Review of Politics

Theory and Society

Third World Quarterly

Western Political Quarterly

Women & Politics

World Policy Journal

World Politics

NEWS SOURCES

General News Links to International Sources:

World Newspapers and Magazines
http://www.world-newspapers.com

Inter Press Service News Agency
http://www.ipsnews.net/http://www.ipsnews.net/

ABYZ News Links
http://www.abyznewslinks.com/

Links to News Sources by Region:

China daily newspapers general website
http://www.onlinenewspapers.com/china.htm

Asia news gateway
http://www.atimes.com/

Latin America news gateway
http://lanic.utexas.edu/la/region/news/

Africa news gateway
http://allafrica.com/

National and International Newspapers:

Christian Science Monitor
http://www.csmonitor.com

The Globe and Mail
http://www.theglobeandmail.com

The Guardian
http://www.guardian.co.uk

Jerusalem Post
http://www.jpost.com

The London Times
http://www.timesonline.co.uk

Le Monde
http://www.lemonde.fr

The Moscow Times
http://www.themoscowtimes.com

National Post
http://nationalpost.com

The New York Times
http://www.nytimes.com

The Washington Post
http://www.washingtonpost.com

POLITICAL SCIENCE SITES FOR STUDENTS

The *Canadian Journal of Political Science* website has a helpful list of guidelines for those wanting to submit papers for publication:
http://www.cpsa-acsp.ca/pdfs/Editorial%20Style%20Guidelines%202008.pdf

Websites with Links to Political Science Sources

Scholarly Societies
http://www.scholarly-societies.org/polisci_soc.html

Research on Various Political Science Topics
http://gsociology.icaap.org/research.html

LIBRARY INDEXES FOR POLITICAL SCIENCE STUDENTS

- Academic Search Complete
- Canadian Newsstand

- Canadian Business and Current Affairs
- CIAO: Columbia International Affairs Online
- IPSA: International Political Science Abstracts
- JSTOR: Journal Storage
- Political Science: Sage Full-Text Collections
- Web of Science (includes a large political science collection)

INFORMATION ON WRITING, RESEARCH, AND CITATION STYLES

WRITING RESOURCES

The Internet has now become the best source for up-to-date information on essay writing. Listed below are several key sites that contain information useful for citation styles, evaluation of electronic sources, and general writing guidelines.

Style Manuals

The American Psychological Association (APA) posts its electronic references style guide online:

http://www.apastyle.org/elecref.html

The Modern Language Association (MLA) homepage contains information on purchasing an MLA Style Guide:

http://www.mla.org

The Chicago Manual of Style's official website:

http://www.chicagomanualofstyle.org/

The following websites contain valuable information on researching, writing, editing, and documenting your sources. Check with these sites to compare styles or get detailed information on how to cite particular items.

Purdue University's Online Writing Lab (OWL)
http://owl.english.purdue.edu

Bedford/St. Martin's Press, sample papers
http://bcs.bedfordstmartins.com/resdoc5e/index.htm

Analyzing Resources
http://www.library.cornell.edu/olinuris/ref/research/skill26.htm

Resources in Print

Buckley, J. (2013). *Fit to print.* Toronto: Nelson.

Concise rules of APA style (6th ed.). (2010). Washington, DC: American Psychological Association.

Finnbogason, J., & Valleau, A. (2011). *A Canadian writer's pocket guide* (4th ed.). Toronto: Nelson.

Hacker, D., & Sommers, N. (2011). *A Canadian writer's reference* (5th ed.). Boston: Bedford/St. Martin's.

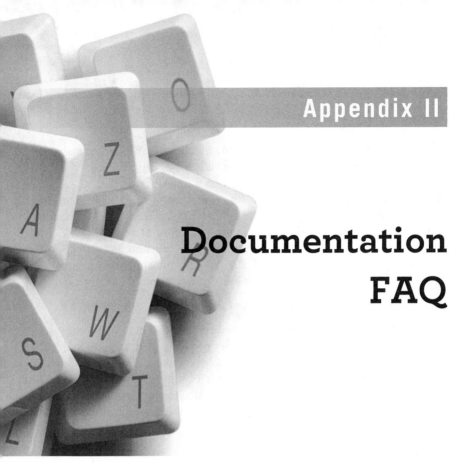

Appendix II

Documentation FAQ

1. Do I have to document every fact?

No, you don't. Do not document general facts that are common knowledge. (Ottawa is the capital of Canada. Stephen Harper won a majority government in May, 2011.)

However, you must give credit for all other information and opinions that do not originate with you. Remember, you are trying to substantiate your own arguments with evidence from others.

2. What are the differences among footnotes, endnotes, and parenthetical documentation?

Footnotes are found at the bottom of a page of printed text and are usually numbered consecutively from the beginning of the unit or chapter. Endnotes are located at the end of a unit of text, such as an article or chapter. They can also be found at the end of a book, where they are usually listed by chapter.

Parenthetical documentation refers to a method of citing the author and work within the text itself, using parentheses to set off information not mentioned in the text. Readers can access the full reference in a reference list at the end of the text. Refer to the section on documentation in Chapter 3 for further information.

3. What are the differences among APA, MLA, and CMS citation styles?

All three are styles of documentation developed by different organizations. The American Psychological Association (APA) developed a slightly different style that is preferred in social science. The Modern Language Association (MLA) developed a system that is used by students and scholars in the humanities. *The Chicago Manual of Style* (CMS) uses both parenthetical documentation and endnotes or footnotes (also called the documentary-note system). Check the list of print and Internet resources in Appendix I for further examples and information.

4. Am I supposed to use a works cited list or a list of references?

It depends on which citation style you are using. The MLA style uses a works cited list. It includes only the titles of works you have quoted, paraphrased, or summarized in the body of your essay. The APA and CMS styles ask for references, so again you put in only those items specifically mentioned in your paper. Some instructors also like to see a separate works consulted list, which gives information on all the research items you read while conducting your research.

5. What is plagiarism?

Plagiarism is a form of cheating. Students and researchers who use part or all of another person's work without giving adequate credit are plagiarizing. Some examples include buying a paper from a term paper service, using the exact words of another person without quotation marks, taking the structure or outline or main points from another work without giving credit, and paraphrasing ideas or writing without citations. Check your institution's policy on plagiarism.

6. What does ibid. mean, and why do I see it in footnotes?

Ibid. is an abbreviation of the Latin word *ibidem*, which means "in the same place." It is frequently used in footnotes and endnotes in a formal style of documentation. *Ibid.* is used for the second reference from the work that appears immediately above it. See examples in Chapter 3.

Many bibliographic citations found in older books and journals use abbreviations and notations taken from Latin. Complete lists can be found by searching under "Latin abbreviations."

7. I'm using parenthetical documentation. Do I have to put the author's name in parentheses if I mentioned her in the text?

No, you don't. The key idea of the author-date system is to streamline references. Any time the documentary information is mentioned in the text, it does not need to be repeated in the parentheses.

8. When do I use quotation marks for source material?

The only time a writer uses quotation marks is when quoting the exact words of another source. Short quotations always need quotation marks. Quotations longer than four lines are set off in a block and do not use quotation marks. Do not use quotation marks for paraphrases. Consult the APA, CMS, and MLA examples in Chapter 3 for more information.

9. What if I can't figure out how to document something?

The guides provided in this manual are general. For more specialized types, please check the websites for the various styles, or consult your instructor. Documenting Internet sources is still a developing area, so instructions may not be consistent. Remember, the goal is to enable the reader to consult all the sources you have used.

COMMON CORRECTION SYMBOLS

Symbols Indicating Problems in Grammar/Expression	Explanation
^	**Omission.** A word or words are missing from the sentence.
agr.	**Error in agreement.** Agreement errors can happen between subjects and verbs and between pronouns and their antecedents. Subjects and verbs must agree in number (singular or plural).
pron. ref.	**Pronoun reference** errors occur when a pronoun does not have a clear noun that it refers to.
X	**Unnecessary word.** Extra words might be a grammar error, such as an extra subject, or just careless proofreading.
id.	**Idiom error.** Idioms must be used in their exact form and for a specific meaning. An instructor may be pointing out an incorrect idiom or the misuse of the idiom for the situation. Many idioms are considered slang and should be improved.
Exp.	**Faulty expression** points to problems with grammar or vocabulary.
∿	**Change the word order.** The notation for changing order can be applied to individual words, phrases, clauses, and sentences.
w.f.	**Word form.** Check the correct word form (noun, verb, adjective, or adverb).
w.w.	**Wrong word.** Some words are easily confused. Other problems are the result of not knowing the correct vocabulary word.
wdy.	**Wordy.** Use clear, direct language without excessive words. Eliminate those expressions that add unnecessary words or phrases.
pass	**Passive voice.** Overuse of the passive voice makes your writing less clear. Although it is not necessary to eliminate all instances of the passive voice, good editing can result in better, more concise language. Check one of the grammar resources listed in this guide for further advice on the passive voice.
frag.	A **fragment** is not a complete sentence. Correct fragments by adding an independent clause or a complete subject and verb.
R.O.	A **run-on sentence** combines too many independent clauses without using conjunctions or subordinate adverbs. In some cases, additional punctuation such as a semicolon or period is the best solution.
C.S.	A **comma splice sentence** contains two independent clauses separated by a comma. Use one of these solutions: (1) change the comma to a period, (2) add a semicolon if the two ideas are related, (3) add a subordinating conjunction, or (4) use a conjunction.
M.M.	**Misplaced modifier.** Modifiers must be clearly connected to the words or phrases they are describing.
//	**Lack of parallelism.** Parallel structure makes sentences sound smoother and clearer. Use the same grammatical structure for words and phrases.